The City of Coral Springs dedicates this book to the people of Coral Springs whose spirit, commitment, and ideals have shaped the community during its first twenty-five years.

CORAL SPRINGS CITY COMMISSION
SILVER ANNIVERSARY YEAR

O.B. "Ben" Geiger
Mayor

Donald H. Sanders
Commissioner

James K. Gordon
Commissioner

Jeanne M. Mills
Commissioner
Elected March 8, 1988

Edward L. Heafy
Commissioner
Retired, March 8, 1988

Janet E. Oppenheimer
Commissioner
Elected March 8, 1988

Helen G. Taché
Commissioner
Retired, March 8, 1988

The city's 20th anniversary celebration at Mullins Park drew a few Coral Springs beauties. Courtesy of City of Coral Springs

The City of Coral Springs expresses its sincere appreciation to the following businesses and organizations that have provided financial support for this book:

Coral Ridge Properties, Inc.
Coral Savings and Loan
Cable TV of Coral Springs
Coral Springs Chamber of Commerce
Southern Bell

CORAL SPRINGS
the first twenty-five years

by Stuart B. McIver

for the

City of Coral Springs

The Donning Company/Publishers
Norfolk, Virginia Beach

The Donning Company/Publishers
Norfolk/Virginia Beach

The annual pumpkin sale draws an interested observer. Courtesy of City of Coral Springs

Copyright © 1988 by The City of Coral Springs, Florida

All rights reserved, including the right to reproduce this work in any form whatsoever without permission in writing from the publisher, except for brief passages in connection with a review. For information, write:

The Donning Company/Publishers
5659 Virginia Beach Boulevard
Norfolk, Virginia 23502

Edited by Nancy O. Phillips
Richard A. Horwege, Senior Editor
Design by Lori Schantz
Cover photo hand colored by Lori Schantz

Library of Congress Cataloging-in-Publication Data

McIver, Stuart B.
   Coral Springs: the first twenty-five years/by Stuart McIver.
   p.   cm.
   "For the city of Coral Springs."
   Includes index.
   ISBN 0-89865-714-8
   1. Coral Springs (Fla.)—History—Pictorial works. 2. Coral Springs (Fla.)—Description—Views. I. Coral Springs (Fla.) II. Title.
F319.C83M37   1988   88-15001
975.9'35—dc 19   CIP

Printed in the United States of America

CONTENTS

Letter from Mayor Geiger 9

Acknowledgments 11

Chapter One
    Two Titans 13

Chapter Two
    Pioneeers, 1960s Style 17

Chapter Three
    Taking Shape 35

Chapter Four
    The Exploding Eighties 53

Chapter Five
    Twenty-five and Counting 81

Chapter Six
    Coral Springs Today 89

Elected and Appointed Officials 121

Milestones 122

Index 123

About the Author 124

At sunset work stops on Sunrise Towers, the city's largest office building. Courtesy of City of Coral Springs

Dear Reader:

Coral Springs: The First Twenty-Five Years will give you an insight into the origin of the City of Coral Springs you never imagined possible. Never before has such an insightful compilation of facts been put into one source. This book will make you proud of your community, and the people who had the foresight to make it happen.

This is the story of a great city, born out of the South's largest string bean fields and pasture land. You will read that once you had to wave a white flag in order to visit what is now Coral Springs because those who guarded the fields had orders to shoot—lest you be mistaken for a cattle rustler.

For those of you new to our city you might find it hard to imagine that the only way into the area twenty-five years ago was via a narrow dirt road called Wiles Road. Nowadays, to get to Coral Springs, one has only to look at a map to discover the myriad of multi-lane superhighways leading into our community.

This informative and picturesque mosaic takes you through the early stages of land acquisition, land rushes, development and gives you a peek at the future.

We hope you enjoy reading and looking back at Coral Springs' first quarter of a century. And, as the old adage goes, "You ain't seen nothing yet!"

O. B. "Ben" Geiger
Mayor

ACKNOWLEDGMENTS

When a city is only twenty-five years old, you have the rare privilege of talking to most of the people who made its history. The list is a long one of people who have helped me with their interviews, photographs, scrapbooks and a wide variety of clippings, brochures and documents on the young city of Coral Springs.

Particular thanks should go to five people without whose help this book could not have been done: Gordon Ickes, one of the town's original settlers, now retired from his vice presidency at Coral Ridge Properties; Jack Gardner, public information officer for the City of Coral Springs, generous with time, information, constructive suggestions, and his excellent photography; Dave Dunleavy, director of visual communications for Coral Ridge Properties; and city commissioner Ed Heafy and his wife Emily. All worked closely with me from the start of the project and were still helping me up till the day the manuscript was shipped to the publisher.

Many others must be thanked: from Coral Ridge Properties, which supplied most of the book's documentation: Matt Wiseley, Roger Turner, Sol Aboulafia, George Hodapp, Jim Novotny and the third and fourth presidents of the company, Bob Hofmann and Werner Buntemeyer.

From the City of Coral Springs, invaluable support was given throughout by Chuck Schwabe, assistant city manager who coordinated the city's participation in the project. Thanks go to a long list of city employees and department heads who helped on many levels: Jack Doughney, Chuck Bull, Gerri Milosevich, Jonda Joseph, Sylvia Starsky, William Brady, Bob David, Buzz Eddy, Jim Miller, Andrea Moore, Dennis Foltz, Sam Stevens, Steven Oxenhandler, Don Eveker, and Warren Gilbert.

Elected officials gave of their time and their counsel: Mayor Ben Geiger and City Commissioners Jim Gordon, Don Sanders, Helen Taché, Janet Oppenheimer, Jeanne Mills, and Senator Peter Weinstein.

Others whose help was vital include Peter Hardiman, Tom Horne, Eugene Andreotti, Donald Jans, Tom Lenz, Rodney Dillon, Bud Thomas, Harvey Olson, Gypsy Graves and Joyce Wente.

Coral Springs is too young to have found its way into very many hardbacked books, but a wealth of information on the city is available through local newspapers, magazines, and promotional materials. Particular thanks go to Joe Nutt and Bob Walton for the 1978 special historical edition of the *Quad City News*. Special editions of the *Coral Springs Forum* and the continuing weekly coverage of the *Coral Springs News* were highly informative, as were the area's daily newspapers, the *Fort Lauderdale News/Sun-Sentinel* and the *Miami Herald*. Magazine stories were consulted from such varied publications as *Fortune, Coral Springs Monthly, Coral Springs Magazine, Florida Parent,* and *Broward Life.*

And finally, a special thanks to the members of the city's Steering Committee for a Twenty-fifth Anniversary Book on Coral Springs, without whose leadership the project could never have been started: Joseph Ash, publisher, Plants, Sites and Parks; Walton A. Orth, Jr., Southern Bell, who served as the Chamber of Commerce's representative; Chuck Schwabe, City of Coral Springs; and Matt Wiseley, vice-president/advertising, Coral Ridge Properties. The story of the birth of a unique city could not have been told without the support of all of the above, who constitute only a small percentage of the many enthusiastic boosters of their hometown, Coral Springs.

From its humble beginnings as swampy Florida ranchland Coral Springs has grown into a city of 75,000 in just a quarter of a century (looking north from C-14 Canal). Courtesy of Coral Ridge Properties.

CHAPTER 1
TWO TITANS

Henry L. (Bud) Lyons saw the vast, empty land in west Broward County as a bean patch; his heirs viewed it, particularly the northwest part, as ranchland. Later, James S. Hunt looked at the open country and saw a city rising from the Everglades, a city he would one day name Coral Springs.

Before World War I Lyons arrived in Pompano as a small boy from Lowndes County, Georgia. By 1919 he was beginning to acquire Broward County farmland. One of his earliest purchases was ninety-nine acres of marshy wilderness west of Pompano. Much of the land he bought was under water, a matted jungle of cypress, myrtle, wild willow and sawgrass, infested with malarial mosquitoes, wildcats, wild hogs, rattlesnakes, water moccasins, and alligators.

Lyons accumulated his land empire bit by bit over many years, sometimes by trading a mule or an old Model T Ford for a piece of land, sometimes by outright purchase. During the Florida land boom of the 1920s he rejected offers for as much as a thousand dollars an acre. Bud wanted more land, not less. After the land boom collapsed in 1926, he set about acquiring more land by buying up property on the delinquent tax rolls. Some of his holdings traced back to the giant, probably illegal, lottery held by Florida Fruit Lands in 1911. This unusual sale was held in Fort Lauderdale, then a frontier settlement, to promote development of the Everglades through the sale of lots.

By the early 1940s Lyons had acquired more than twenty thousand acres between Fort Lauderdale and the Palm Beach County line, stretching west from Route 441 deep into the Everglades. A 1939 article in the *Country Home Magazine* declared he had become "probably the biggest individual string bean grower in America." The magazine dubbed him the "Titan of the Bean Patch."

A tough-minded, independent man, he set about draining the land himself. "If the state reclaims the land for me," he said, "I'll pay for it in taxes. I'll do my own reclaiming."

The Titan built channels, ditches, locks, and levees. He installed diesel-driven pumps for his sixty miles of waterways. Dry land emerged from the Everglades. To burn off vegetation and clear the land, he brought in a hundred black laborers from the Bahamas. Draglines and one of the nation's few tree-dozers roared into action. Tractors and plows prepared the land for planting. Bud Lyons, the Titan, had transformed virgin marshland into fertile farm land. Each year it yielded two crops of winter vegetables for shipment to the North and the Middle West.

In 1939 Lyons began to experiment with a breed of cattle new to the area, the Brahman, hardy enough to withstand the heat and the insects of the Florida Everglades. When Bud died in 1952, his descendants felt the time had come to convert much of his giant bean patch into a ranch. Five thousand head of cattle, mostly Brahman, grazed on Lyons land, particularly in northwest Broward. There the soil had always been marginal as farmland.

With the switch to ranching the threats to the Lyons family enterprise were no longer frost, flooding, and hurricanes. Now they faced a meaner foe—rustlers. Cattle thieves invaded the Lyons domain. So did hunters, who cut down fences, shot the locks off gates, and then killed deer, wildcats, and wild hogs, and not infrequently Lyons cattle.

The family name portrayed strength, and it asserted itself quickly. The Lyons interests quickly organized armed posses. Men with shotguns and rifles patrolled the ranch in pickups, roaming around some sixty miles of dirt roads that Bud had built. West Broward had become the Wild West.

But momentous events had been set in motion that would transform West Broward again to a world

Henry L. (Bud) Lyons, "the Titan of the Bean Patch," sits at his office desk in Pompano (about 1938). Courtesy of Broward County Historical Commission

Bud Lyons would never have envisaged. Two years after the series of wet hurricanes and floods in 1947, state and federal money had been poured into the creation of the Central and Southern Florida Flood Control District (FCD), now known as the South Florida Water Management District. The FCD built a mammoth network of canals, levees and pumping stations throughout a vast expanse of Florida and, in particular, in the area south of Lake Okeechobee. All over West Broward dry land began to emerge and developers looked out over the Everglades and saw raw land to be converted into communities, towns, and cities.

From Fort Lauderdale the bean patch's second titan was about to make his entrance. James S. Hunt, a child of the city, urbane, sophisticated, and dapper down to the tips of his pencil-thin mustache, was an unlikely successor to the mantle worn by country boy Bud Lyons, but he proved to be the right man for the times. Hunt had honed his considerable selling skills in the automobile business in Detroit. At one time he was the country's largest Chevrolet dealer.

After World War II Hunt came to Fort Lauderdale, where he decided to enter the real estate development field. With two partners, Joseph Taravella, who had served under him in the Navy during the war, and Stephen Calder, a Fort Lauderdale real estate man since the boom days of the 1920s, he formed a new company. Since the land they were developing lay along the coral ridge in northeast Fort Lauderdale, they called the company Coral Ridge Properties (CRP).

From Sunrise Boulevard to Pompano Beach, Coral Ridge Properties developed an area containing some eight thousand homes and seven thousand luxury oceanfront apartments. In 1953 CRP put together the largest land transaction ever completed in the United States at that time. For $19,389,000 the company bought nearly twenty-five hundred acres from Arthur Galt of Chicago. Part of it would become the Galt Ocean Mile, a string of luxury, high-rise condominiums facing the Atlantic. In the 1920s land boom, Galt had sold the land to Gwendolyn Maitland, the Scottish Countess of Lauderdale. Galt then took the land back after the real estate collapse of 1926.

By the early 1960s Hunt and his staff were looking at a problem no developer likes to confront. They were beginning to run short of land to develop. Like Bud Lyons before him, Hunt liked to paint on a large canvas. He was not interested in small subdivisions. He wanted enough land to create a city, enough land to design and control the look of the entrances to his city, enough land to buffer its residential areas from noise and unpleasant vistas. No such parcel of land existed anywhere in east Broward County. To find the land he wanted, Hunt had to do exactly what Lyons did—go west. The paths of Jim Hunt and Bud Lyons were about to cross.

Bud's widow, Lena Lyons, had become a classic example of being "land poor." Farm and ranching income had declined, but property taxes went on and on. She had more land than she needed, more than she wanted. What she wanted was cash.

Who had enough money to pay her what she wanted? Who had reason to buy land from her? Certainly not other farmers or ranchers. But developers, there was another matter. Since 1950, nine new towns had been incorporated west of State Road 7. Lena's brother, Louis Fisher, concluded that Hunt was her best target.

The talks began in the summer of 1961 at CRP's small office on North Federal Highway, Fort Lauderdale. Hunt was interested, but negotiations did not come easily. Lena Lyons was a shrewd, tough bargainer. She knew what she wanted and she was prepared to hold out for it.

Inspecting the land was difficult. The elegant Hunt was not a man to cruise the Wild West in a pickup truck or don dungarees and boots to slog his way through marsh and jungle. So clothes-conscious was Hunt that friends had nicknamed him "Esky" after the cartoon character who had become the trademark for fashion-conscious *Esquire* magazine. Hunt sent two of his top executives, Joseph Taravella and Robert Hofmann, who had joined the company in 1947.

Bud Lyons used his vast West Broward lands for more than raising beans and herding cattle. Before the land became Coral Springs, the Titan, at the right, also used it for deer hunting for friends and family. Just right of Bud Lyons is his father, Church Lyons. Courtesy of Broward County Historical Commission

Lena Lyons beamed when James S. Hunt, president of Coral Ridge Properties, handed her a check for $1 million. For his million Hunt acquired thirty-eight hundred acres of land in northwest Broward County. The land would become the start of Coral Springs. Courtesy of Coral Ridge Properties

The only way into the property was over a narrow, dirt strip, called Wiles Road. It could be reached only from State Road 7, itself a dirt road at the time. When Taravella and Hofmann reached Wiles Road, they had to wave a large white flag, a signal to the armed posses that someone wanted to visit the property. Since Lena's roving bands had orders to shoot rustlers, visitors found it desirable to follow whatever routine Lena wanted. Only after they produced acceptable identification were Taravella and Hoffman allowed to travel the rough dirt roads that intersected the cattle empire.

What they saw was less than impressive. It did, however, fill Hunt's requirement for a vast tract of land. Unfortunately, much of it was swampland. Just beneath the surface an extensive caprock held water after the county's numerous rains. Still, the land was high by Florida standards—twelve to fourteen feet in places—and there was plenty of it. Enough land for the company to lay out streets, parks, business and industrial zones and, most important of all to a real estate developer, large residential subdivisions.

Lena Lyons and CRP talked about a 3,860-acre parcel of land. Bud Lyons had rejected an offer of a thousand dollars an acre for land some four decades earlier. Lena was also negotiating another deal, for 20 acres at two thousand dollars an acre. When this deal fell through, she was suddenly strapped for cash.

Hunt offered her $259 an acre for 3,860 acres. "You've got a week to decide, or I knock a quarter of a million off the price," he told her.

Within a week Lena returned and accepted the offer—but with an unusual stipulation.

"I want to do something for my kinfolks for Christmas," she said. "We've got to close by then."

Hunt knew it was an almost impossible task to complete so large a transaction by then. Bud had accumulated his land from so many sources that the title searches led through a maze of old tax bills and deeds that dated back to the bizarre frontier land lottery of 1911. But lawyers from both camps pitched in, and on December 14, 1961, just before Christmas, James Hunt handed Lena Lyons an impressive present—a check for one million dollars.

Lena Handed him an even more impressive present—the land that would become Coral Springs.

Gordon Ickes, director of advertising and public relations, was one of the original CRP employees moved to the developer's northwest Broward land to qualify the new settlement for incorporation. It was primitive living, amidst rattlesnakes, wildcats and stampeding cattle, but the signs indicate Ickes kept his sense of humor. Courtesy of Coral Ridge Properties

CHAPTER 2
PIONEERS, 1960s STYLE

"George, I want you to do some thinking about what to do with this land," said James Hunt. For young George Hodapp, just one year out of the University of Miami with a degree in architectural engineering, it would prove to be a formidable challenge. For one thing, not even Hunt (the "Old Man," as his staff called him) knew just what direction the new town would take.

All agreed that the property fulfilled the oft-repeated developer's cliche that the three most important virtues of any piece of real estate were location, location, and location. It lay in the northern part of Broward, the middle county among the three which comprised Florida's glamorous and prestigious Gold Coast. In fact, one of the company's earliest advertising slogans was "the Last Piece of Gold on the Gold Coast." The tract was only fifteen miles from Fort Lauderdale, less than that from Boca Raton, and less than fifty miles from Palm Beach and Miami.

Hunt's first thought had been to create a retirement city, as most of the other communities in West Broward were becoming. Under consideration was a retirement village for National Maritime Union members. It would have been named Curran Village after William Curran, the hot-tempered Irishman who headed the militant union. The talks broke off and Hunt sought another avenue—and another name.

For a while the development was called Quartermore. If a buyer purchased three acres of land, another acre, or a "quarter more," was thrown in with the deal. Pompano Springs was considered, and rejected, but the suggestion spun off the name that caught on—Coral Springs. It combined part of the company name with a tribute to the waters that would lie over all too much of the land until a more effective drainage program could be devised.

Once the name was chosen, CRP proceeded with plans to incorporate the new town. Incorporation required a city charter and a minimum of five people living on the land where the city would eventually rise.

Hunt chose the Fort Lauderdale city charter as his model. By simply substituting "Coral Springs" for "Fort Lauderdale," the company came up with an acceptable document. Most of the provisions applied well enough to the new city except for mysterious clauses regulating railroads, which were nowhere near the community, and the seaport, which lay a good twenty-five miles from landlocked Coral Springs.

To create instant population for Coral Springs, the company bought three wooden houses, really little more than shacks, and had them towed north on State Road 7 and west on Wiles Road to today's Riverside Drive. There they were positioned to gain fleeting fame as the town's first homes.

Recruited to move in as the pioneer settlers of Coral Springs were Gordon Ickes, James Novotny, George Porter, and Val Baker, all employees of Coral Ridge Properties. Since Novotny was married and had a son, David, the instant colony contained enough residents to qualify as an incorporated municipality.

On July 10, 1963, Coral Springs was officially chartered by special act of the Florida legislature. The legislature also created the Sunshine Drainage District to manage the drainage of the new town, which now contained five thousand acres after the first of two additional land purchases from Lena Lyons. The Sunshine Drainage District functioned as a public corporation, administered by a board of commissioners and a district supervisor appointed by the governor of Florida. Another company employee, Werner Buntemeyer, a native of Germany, was named to head the district.

What was life like for those hardy pioneers? Said Ickes, a former resident of Springfield, Illinois, and a grandnephew of Harold Ickes, the famous secretary of the interior during the administration of Franklin D.

Work was under way in 1964 on a major north-south road to be named University Drive. Plans called for it to reach all the way from the University of Miami to Florida Atlantic University in Boca Raton. This scene looks south on University at its intersection with Sample Road. Courtesy of Coral Ridge Properties

Roosevelt:

"It was scary. You saw or you heard wild cats, foxes, rattlers, a lot of deer. I never saw one but I saw panther footprints."

Jim Novotny, who had come to Florida from New England, recalls Hurricane Cleo, which swept through the area in 1964:

"All the houses were tied down except one, the big house with columns. The corner kept lifting up and down."

Hurricanes were only occasional visitors. Wildlife was around all the time. Jim Novotny recalled:

"We had one 120-foot well for all the houses. One time we couldn't get any water and couldn't figure out just why. It turned out a coral snake got into the control box and shorted out the pump." The coral snake is the most poisonous of all Florida reptiles.

Meanwhile Hodapp continued to wrestle with a variety of questions. Where to locate future streets, drainage canals and subdivisions? How big should the lots be? Where should commercial areas be? How much land for parks? In 1963 he drew up a plat for the city's first subdivision, adapted from a plat the company had done for a section of Fort Lauderdale called Coral Ridge Isles. Carved out of acreage bought from Lena Lyons, it would in time become the Meadows.

By 1964 the master plan projected a city of over fifty thousand people, to be developed in three concurrent phases: a retirement apartment village of thirty-seven hundred condominium garden apartments, to be named Coral Springs Village; a series of urban subdivisions; and Coral Springs Hills, a section of one- to two-acre parcels for ranch estates. The initial plan called for thirty miles of roads and thirty miles of canals within an area partly defined by Wiles Road on the north and three streets that existed then only on paper: Sample Road, Woodside Drive, and Riverside Drive. Initial land improvements were budgeted at $3.1 million.

In April 1964 the company unveiled its dream to Broward real estate brokers. A bus tour of the State Road 7 and Wiles Road area was conducted for real estate professionals, who saw little except a vast, open tract of land. The company's sales force, however, made sure that they heard mesmerizing words about a great city that would arise in northwest Broward.

After tantalizing the brokers with the bus tours, Coral Ridge Properties held a giant land-sales meeting on July 22 at the Galt Ocean Mile Hotel, an oceanfront Fort Lauderdale hotel owned by the company. On the block was Coral Springs Subdivision No. 1. It was called the first urban subdivision, even though traces of urban civilization were scarce in a land of wildcats and rattlesnakes.

A standing-room-only crowd of fifteen hundred brokers showed up. Hunt, a salesman without peer, was ready with dancing girls, Dixieland bands, slide presentations and bargain discounts, all orchestrated to bring the brokers charging forward with checkbooks. After the pitch the brokers had just fourteen minutes to take advantage of the company's pre-development prices. In that tightly compressed envelope of opportunity, brokers moved quickly to pay $1.6 million for 536 building lots. Coral Springs was on its way.

In developing the Coral Ridge section of Fort Lauderdale, Hunt had learned the value of restrictive covenants in controlling the look and style of his communities. CRP was not basically a builder but rather a developer of lots and parcels to be sold to builders for residential and commercial construction. Builders who bought from CRP both in Fort Lauderdale and later in Coral Springs were restricted by a variety of stipulations as to size, type and cost of houses; size of residential lots; setback from streets; and size and appearance of signs in the community.

To his new city, Hunt wanted to bring the look of Old Virginia—white columns, red brick, verandas, maybe even a magnolia or two.

"The Old Man liked Dixie," said Ickes. "Coral Springs was going to be the Old South. Once he loaded the whole staff into a bus on a hot summer day and took us up into Georgia to get the smell of mint and see the homes with columns. He even decided a covered bridge looked southern."

Hunt called Hodapp into his office. "George, we need a covered bridge."

"A what?"

"I want a covered bridge and I want you to build it."

Fort Lauderdale real estate brokers gathered at the Galt Ocean Mile Hotel to buy the first lots in the Coral Springs land sale on July 22, 1964. Left to right are Max Welborn, George Collier and Fred Shimpf. Courtesy of Coral Ridge Properties

Brokers contest hotly for discounts on land at the Coral Springs land sale. Courtesy of Coral Ridge Properties

One purpose of the bridge was to carry traffic north and south on Northwest Ninety-fifth Avenue in the Hills subdivision, south of Wiles Road. The other purpose was to serve as a landmark in a town that had very few distinctive features. Although nearly all of America's covered bridges were built in the nineteenth century, Hodapp had little trouble designing a steel span forty feet long with a vertical clearance of ten feet, four inches. Its wooden superstructure made it the only covered bridge in Florida. The bridge was built by contractor George Porter and Lewie Mullins, both CRP employees.

The structure worked as a bridge, but to qualify as a landmark, it needed more character than a red paint job could deliver. Hunt had seen a chewing tobacco sign on a covered bridge with just the touch he wanted, old-fashioned but still southern. He called the chairman of the board of the American Snuff Company in Atlanta and asked him to put a tobacco sign on a new covered bridge in Coral Springs.

"We haven't had a request like that for a hundred and fifty years," Hunt was told. But the chairman was delighted. He came down personally to supervise the production of the signs, boosting two of his company's products: Peach Sweet Snuff ("Sweet as a Peach") and Bull of the Woods chewing tobacco. Later the International Organization for the Preservation of Covered Bridges sent down a deputation to inspect America's newest covered bridge.

When it was built, the covered bridge sat out in the open, in solitary splendor. Still, it gave Hunt what he wanted—a landmark, something unique his new town could claim. In time the twentieth-century covered bridge would be used for the Coral Springs logo.

The first building constructed in Coral Springs was a small wooden sales headquarters in the corner of State Road 7 and Wiles Road.

Activity in 1964 was so low that the company had to staff the city administration. Tapped for the job of first city manager was one of its staff, Werner Buntemeyer. He would hold the post until 1974 and later rise to the presidency of the company. In addition to his duties with CRP, he ran the city and the Sunshine Drainage District. A district bond issue for $2,131,000 financed the cost of dredging C-14, the master canal on the south side of Coral Springs, and the additional network of canals and pumping station needed for effective drainage.

Since the new property owners were reluctant to build at first, eight southern colonial-style models were built in the Meadows subdivision on lots CRP had retained from its first land sale. Early traffic was slow, as were sales.

To provide a southern entrance into Coral Springs, the company bought four hundred acres from Rodman Rockefeller just west of Margate. On this land the company built the Royal Palm Boulevard gateway into Coral Springs.

In 1965 Hunt went back to Lena Lyons again and picked up an additional five thousand acres. These increased the company's holdings to more than sixteen square miles. At that point Coral Springs had the third largest land area in Broward County, exceeded only by Fort Lauderdale, with 29.9 square

The Covered Bridge spans a canal on Northwest Ninety-fifth Avenue (Covered Bridge Drive) in the Hills, a subdivision just south of Wiles Road. Now the symbol of Coral Springs, the bridge was built in 1964 by Lewie Mullins, George Porter, and Jim Novotny. Courtesy of Coral Ridge Properties

miles, and Hollywood, with 24.

By now a master plan for Coral Springs was beginning to emerge. Hodapp was working closely with Hayden Benning Associates, a planning firm from the Maryland suburbs of Washington. Roads were laid out by the West Palm Beach engineering company, Gee & Jensen. For esthetic reasons the company wanted curving roads where possible, a position opposed by the Broward County Area Planning Board, which found straight roads better for traffic flow.

"Hunt wanted to build something unusual and the straight line ruled that out," recalled Hodapp. "Buford Hayden was able to make a strong case for curving roads in the southern part of the town. He cited the need to avoid wetlands and other natural features the county wanted to preserve anyway."

Early plans showed wide streets and wide setbacks, parks, and commercial and industrial sections. Land was even designated for a regional mall almost two decades before it became a reality. The original plan for what is now Eagle Trace appeared first as "Village IX," an area of high-rise multifamily dwellings.

The look of the town was being established through strict sign and landscaping ordinances and deed restrictions. The city's tough sign policy was adapted from the signage ordinance for Honolulu, which Hodapp had visited on his way back from service in the Korean War.

As a cattle ranch, the land had been stripped of vegetation. Extensive new planting was required, but the ordinance banned such undesirable exotics as malaleuca, Brazilian pepper, Australian pine, and eucalyptus. On land the company controlled, the CRP planning department was required to approve every set of plans for building and landscaping.

Nine million dollars expended for development put Coral Ridge Properties in position for its second big land sale in March 1965. This time the sale could be held in the new town in northwest Broward County, a town that was no longer just on paper. Now there were roads, five and a half miles of them, and waterways and model homes built for the event.

It was billed as the state's "largest LAND-RUSH Discount Land Sale and Barbecue." And what a

Work began on the Broken Woods golf course as the new city started to take shape. At left center the clubhouse can be seen. Courtesy of Coral Ridge Properties

Preparations were extensive for the huge discount land sale at Coral Springs in March 1965. The house at the left is a model near the Covered Bridge. The Coral Ridge Properties salesmen in the picture are Bob Hartford, second from right, and Carlton (Monty) Montayne, at far left. Monty became the first manager of the Coral Springs Chamber of Commerce. Courtesy of Coral Ridge Properties

Visitors arriving for the discount land sale drove across the Covered Bridge (right center) to reach the seats in front of the stage. By the time the sale started, ten thousand people were on hand. Courtesy of Coral Ridge Properties

"Here's Johnny" could have been the call from Harry Wilson, left, first mayor of Coral Springs, to Johnny Carson, at right. Carson, already well on his way to becoming a television celebrity as host of NBC's "Tonight Show," was the star who helped lure the crowds to the land sale. To Johnny's right is orchestra leader Guy Lombardo, who was in town playing an engagement at a Fort Lauderdale hotel owned by Coral Ridge Properties. Courtesy of Coral Ridge Properties

Cheerleaders whoop it up for the big Coral Springs land sale of 1965. Courtesy of Coral Ridge Properties

production it was! Some 350 people, 30,000 man hours and $100,000 were poured into the planning and preparation.

The event called for entertainment to draw a big crowd. Drum majorettes, cheerleaders and Scottish bagpipers were brought in, but just to make sure the promotion packed them in, two celebrities—Guy Lombardo and Johnny Carson—were recruited. Guy Lombardo was already in the area with his orchestra, playing "the sweetest music this side of heaven" at CRP's Galt Ocean Mile Hotel. Lombardo made the trip out to Coral Springs, as did Carson, then a young TV personality just beginning to emerge as a star on NBC's "Tonight Show." In a Rolls Royce Johnny Carson led the motorcade up State Road 7 to Wiles Road and west to the site of the land sale.

Ten thousand people showed up, 150 of them land brokers. It took three tons of barbecue and three tons of hot dogs—two miles' worth—and twenty-five hundred gallons of soft drinks to feed and slake the thirst of the crowd.

There was really very little for them to see—a vast and open land, a few miles of roads, and a handful of model homes. These lonely components, however, were richly seasoned with a torrent of good, old-fashioned salesmanship. Soon the guests were seeing and hearing a vision of a bustling, thriving city of some sixty thousand people, living in a town of spacious lots, parks, and wide streets.

E. O. (Chubby) Knight sold eleven hundred lots that day, comprising three hundred acres, for $5 million. Seven hundred and fifty of these were sold in the thirty-minute period when lots were offered at discounts ranging from one-fourth to one-third off the listed price. Homesites in the Meadows sold for $2,695 and up; in the Hills for $9,000 and up; in the Country Club area for $7,500 and up; and in the Village Green for $5,500 and up. Home prices for the models in the Meadows ranged from $15,000 to $20,000. In the Coral

Real estate brokers wearing cowboy hats push forward to buy land which a few years earlier had been a cattle ranch. Courtesy of Coral Ridge Properties

James Hunt even talked a young Johnny Carson into buying 54.6 acres of Coral Springs land along Royal Palm Boulevard. In 1970 Johnny sold it for five times what he paid for it six years earlier. Courtesy of Coral Ridge Properties

Springs Country Club area, home prices started at $15,000 and in the Hills at $20,000.

Early models were built by the company to awaken interest in the new city. After the land rush, other builders began to construct homes for the future residents of Coral Springs.

The first house sold by CRP in Coral Springs was bought by George Knobel, a retiree from the U.S. Air Force. He moved into his new home at 4134 Northwest Seventy-eighth Lane on July 9, 1965. The three-bedroom, two-bath house cost $21,100, including a swimming pool and screened patio. Its assessment today is between $80,000 and $100,000.

"I had just retired from the Air Force," Knobel says. "I had a horse, and I was looking for a place in the country. I saw the projections and I thought it was a growing community."

By September it was indeed a growing community, as well as a busy and noisy one. The sounds of saws and hammers mingled with the roar of earth-moving and dredging equipment. Preliminary work had begun on two golf courses, the executive course called Broken Woods and the championship course at the Coral Springs Country Club, designed by Edward Ault, who had created over a hundred courses around the world.

Still, with all the bustle and noise Coral Springs remained a very small town. Its official population in 1965 was listed as just ten people. Some, however, suspected that the actual number approached fifty.

The large lots and open country made the new town an ideal spot for horse owners like George Knobel, and a "horsey set" quickly discovered the virtues of Coral Springs' spacious lots. Four benefit horse shows were held, with the proceeds going to the Broward County School for Retarded Children.

Governor Farris Bryant named Harry W. Wilson the town's first mayor. Rounding out the first commission were George W. Hammerer, vice-mayor,

An open field lay where the Coral Springs Post Office stands today on 94th Avenue near Coral Hills Drive. Courtesy of Coral Ridge Properties

In 1965 Richard Vedilago was named the city's first police chief. He was backed up by a patrol car and a police dog named Sergeant Satan. Courtesy of Coral Ridge Properties

Golfers tee off at Broken Woods, the first Coral Springs golf course. Courtesy of Coral Ridge Properties

and Kenneth W. Pezoldt, Thomas Jarrell Alexander and Harvey Olsen, Jr., commissioners. In October the mayor appointed a three-member planning board "to maintain proper city planning in light of the anticipated growth."

In November Coral Springs responded to one of the harsher realities of population growth. Richard Vedilago was named as the city's first police chief. That same month twenty-seven voters—freeholders—participated in the town's first bond referendum. They voted twenty-five to two for a $12.5-million water and sewer bond issue, plus two hundred thousand dollars for streets, to be paid for by ad valorem taxes.

The years from 1963 to 1965 had set the stage for the emergence of the new city. Now the pace began to quicken. In April 1966, Florida governor Haydon Burns officiated at the opening of the CRP Administration Building at 9500 West Sample Road (built, of course, in colonial style). That same month golfers teed off for the first nine holes of the Broken Woods Golf Course. In June the first U.S. Post Office opened, with Dorothy Conncrs the first postmistress and Caroline Mullins the assistant postmistress.

In the late 1950s Westinghouse Electric Corporation had become interested in Coral Ridge Properties. CRP, it was said, had been the country's largest buyer of General Electric appliances for its Fort Lauderdale developments, particularly on the Galt Ocean Mile. Westinghouse sent representatives to try to sell CRP their line of electrical products. They did more than sell. They wound up buying Coral Ridge Properties on July 1, 1966, for $36 million.

Westinghouse wanted to create an urban laboratory to evaluate new products, such as a home utility center, home sewage disposal systems, an infrared heating system, full electric kitchens and central air-conditioning and heating systems. The company also proposed the construction of a $5-million, 150,000-square-foot plant to manufacture radar control systems and products for defense and aerospace projects. The plant, set on a 350-acre site in the Coral Springs Industrial Park, would employ five hundred persons.

Not the least of the acquisition's attractions to Westinghouse was CRP's record of having made money every year since its founding. Its 1965 annual report listed net income of $1,657,916 on total revenues of $9,057,013.

On July 5, 1966, Mayor Harry Wilson officiated at the dedication of Royal Palm Boulevard, now completed through Margate at a cost of four hundred thousand dollars. Palm trees planted in the median strip promised visitors an attractive gateway into Coral Springs as well as a savings of five to ten minutes' driving time from the south.

In January of 1967 the Coral Springs Chamber of Commerce was organized. Carlton (Monty) Montayne, a CRP real estate salesman, was picked to manage the chamber. Among the subjects discussed at the chamber's first meeting were school sites; new business prospects, including "a service station, larger restaurant, and a Boston Rug store"; city beautification; and the possibility of a city library in the chamber's offices in the Administration Building.

Werner Buntemeyer, city manager, left, meets with the first Coral Springs mayor, Harry Wilson, second from right. Others in the picture are attorney Steve Beyer, at left, George Russell, at Wilson's right, and Hal Byrum, at right. Courtesy of Coral Ridge Properties

By the end of 1967 growth had reached the point where the residents were ready for their first election. One hundred and ninety-five citizens elected Lewie Mullins mayor and Robert J. Fuller vice-mayor. Named to the city commission were Wilfred Neale, Peter Giordano, and Richard J. Hunt.

Even as the town was beginning to grow, an event occurred in early 1967 that briefly focused not on the glowing future of planners and salesmen, but on a long distant past.

Wilma Williams, head of the Broward County Archeological Society, a small group of volunteer diggers, came to Gordon Ickes with an unexpected

In 1966 work was completed on the Administration Building. It would serve first as corporate headquarters for Coral Ridge Properties and later as Coral Springs City Hall. Courtesy of Coral Ridge Properties

"A bit of Old Virginia" in the form of the Administration Building beckons to a youthful group of equestrian enthusiasts. Courtesy of Coral Ridge Properties

request. Far west, just south of what would one day be Sample Road, local archeologists had located an Indian mound. They wanted a chance to excavate before development reached the area.

Ickes was intrigued with the idea. He had the land cleared for the archeologists and an access road built to the area. Then he went them one better, joining them with a shovel and proceeding to dig with the archeologists into the 80-by-112-foot black dirt mound.

Six months of digging produced some interesting results. Tequesta Indians had lived in the area as long ago as 1500 B.C. Located within eight burial sites were picks and awls made of shell, bone arrow points, beads, human teeth, stone and bone artifacts and sharks' teeth, a reminder that once the entire Florida peninsula was under water.

Of particular interest was the discovery of a small religious silver pendant, clearly of Spanish origin. After consultation with many authorities, including a professor from the University of Barcelona, Broward archeologists concluded it was made during or before the seventeenth century for the Order of Our Lady of Mercy. Did the medal indicate that Spaniards had once camped in Coral Springs? Probably not. It was felt that more likely the medal was given to a Tequesta who had been converted to the Catholic faith and then had brought it back to his village.

A later dig at what became Mullins Park yielded bones of ancient mammoths, camels, giant sloths, turtles, alligators, and horses, with some bones dating back ten thousand years.

It was a good thing that the archeologists had completed their dig at the Indian mound in the summer of 1967. The following year the Broward County Commission decided that the growth of Coral Springs justified extending Sample Road on past the Indian mound, out to the levee at Everglades Conservation Area No. 2.

Joe Taravella, who had succeeded Hunt as president of Coral Ridge Properties, unveiled Westinghouse's new Electra Lab Concept in January of 1969. CRP would develop a clustered community which would provide "a practical proving ground in the market place of public acceptance for innovative products and systems, as well as land planning, and provide the means of computerized testings to determine which products, systems and equipment are the most effective and profitable for future use."

Westinghouse built a theme house in the Electra Lab section just south of Sample Road. As many as four thousand people visited the house one weekend to see such novel products as push-button drapes, smoke sensors, window and door security sensors, remote-control TV, and an electronic sewage disposal unit.

Plans for the large Westinghouse plant in the Park of Industry had meanwhile run into problems. The plant, which had been scaled back to a hundred thousand square feet, had been designated to manufacture torpedoes for the Navy. Unfortunately, Westinghouse had not been awarded the contract. Not until 1975 would the plant be utilized. At that time the Burroughs Corporation would purchase it for its incoding/imaging division.

The first operating industry within the Park of

The first Coral Springs post office opened on June 1, 1966, in the east wing of the Coral Ridge Properties Administration Building. Left to right are Dorothy Connors, first postmistress, and Mrs. Lewie Mullins, her assistant. Courtesy of Coral Ridge Properties

In September 1967, the Village Green Shopping Center, a "Williamsburg-style" complex, opened with a number of basic urban services—a pharmacy, a market, a restaurant and lounge, and a barber shop. Courtesy of Coral Ridge Properties

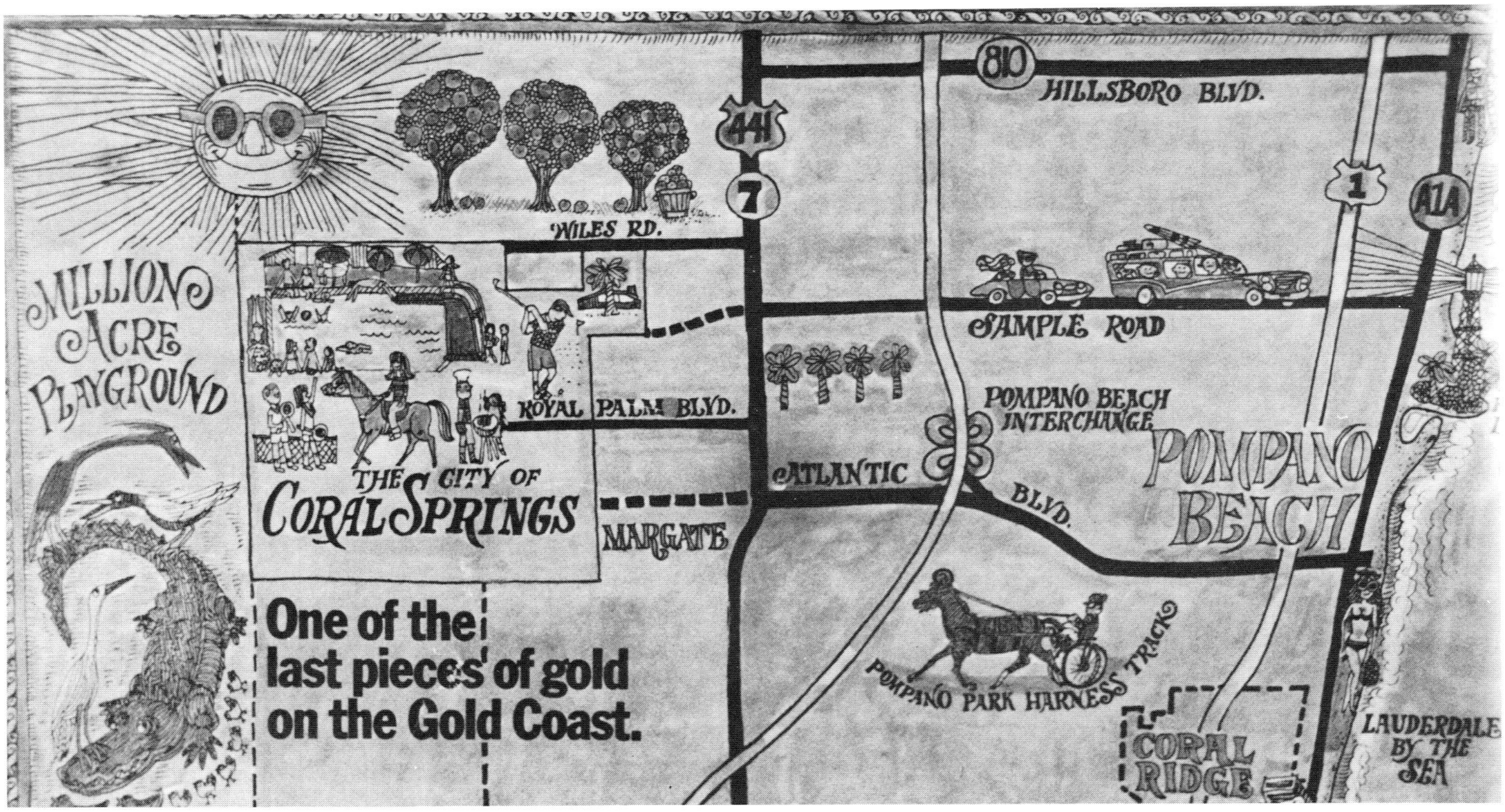

![Map artwork with slogan "One of the last pieces of gold on the Gold Coast."]

One of the earliest slogans used to sell Coral Springs was the phrase, "One of the last pieces of gold on the Gold Coast." This artwork was used by Harvey Olsen, whose advertising agency handled the Coral Ridge Properties account. Olsen, who was a city commissioner and later vice-mayor, served in World War II with unusual distinction. While with the Office of Strategic Services (which later became the CIA), he turned his artistic skills to forgery and counterfeiting to confuse the Nazis. He and his son designed the official logo of the city of Coral Springs. Courtesy of Coral Ridge Properties

The Red Fox Inn on Sample Road was the first hangout for the movers and shakers of the new city. Courtesy of Ed and Emily Heafy

Industry was New Industrial Techniques, an innovative firm which used advanced powder metallurgy for fabricating parts for computers, copiers and business machines. Eugene Andreotti, president, started with seven employees in May of 1969. In less than two decades the company grew to 230 employees.

By the end of the decade thirty-three independent builders were operating in Coral Springs. Home costs were now averaging thirty-five to forty thousand dollars, with some homes running as high as a quarter million. Apartment construction was moving ahead with over 180 condominium units under construction in two four-story and two ten-story buildings.

In response to the population growth, police chief Vedilago's force expanded to six men and added two new Oldsmobile Delta 88 cruisers.

A sad note for 1969 was the October death of the city's first elected mayor, Lewie Mullins. Two months later city commissioners Raymond Lopez and Wilfred Neale presented a plan for the first phase of a large public park on part of a twenty-acre site donated to the city by Coral Ridge Properties. The park would be known as Mullins Park.

Earth-moving equipment goes into action at Sherwood Forest, one of the early Coral Springs subdivisions. Courtesy of Coral Ridge Properties

At Broken Woods Estates homes feature large family rooms, central air conditioning, marble tile baths and sunken living rooms. Courtesy of Coral Ridge Properties

At Broken Woods Estates in 1967, houses on quarter-acre lots could be bought for twenty-five to thirty thousand dollars. Courtesy of Coral Ridge Properties

Employees of Coral Ridge Properties gather on Employees Day to watch the 1967 raising of the Westinghouse flag. Across the street sits a Gulf station, built in the Old Virginia rather than the classic Gulf style, a result of the pressure of Jim Hunt's signage covenants. Courtesy of Coral Ridge Properties

In 1968 Westinghouse was building the first plant in the Park of Industry. It would later be sold to the Burroughs Corporation. Courtesy of Coral Ridge Properties

Coral Springs young people joined members of the Broward County Archeological Society in a dig at a Tequesta Indian mound, south of Sample Road near the levee. Found in the dig were tools, arrowheads and bone fragments, indicating Indian habitation in the area some three thousand years ago. Courtesy of Coral Ridge Properties

Westinghouse opened its Experimental Home of the Future in 1969. The house, which drew four thousand visitors one weekend, demonstrated such advanced products as push-button drapes and window and door security sensors. Courtesy of Coral Ridge Properties

In the spring of 1969 a different kind of model home appeared in Coral Springs. Its builders, Atlantic Construction Co., called the house "the Russian Home." Built in the Dells subdivision from plans published in a Soviet journal on housing, the Russian Home proved effective in attracting visitors to its "American Home" models. Courtesy of Coral Ridge Properties

In 1969 work was proceeding on the new Coral Springs County Club golf course. Courtesy of Coral Ridge Properties

In 1970 Publix broke ground for a supermarket, but before then served Coral Springs with leased space in the Village Green shopping center. It was called the smallest Publix in the world. Courtesy of Coral Ridge Properties

CHAPTER 3
TAKING SHAPE

Coral Springs, a new town which did not exist when the 1960s began, could point to a total of 1,489 residents in the official United States Census of 1970. Werner Buntemeyer felt that was a bit low. He estimated a population of 3,750.

As it entered its first full decade, the city began to take shape. It had been chartered, platted, and planned, and now families were locating in the single-family homes builders were busily erecting. Residents were just beginning to occupy the city's first high-rise condominium, the ten-story Briarwood. The city had a drainage system, a water and sewer facility, and a few streets and roads. An infrastructure was now in place.

Two hundred and sixty-nine voters had named a new city commission to take office in January 1970. George MacGregor was elected mayor; Wilfred Neale, vice-mayor; and James Edwards, Richard J. Hunt, and Edward L. Heafy, commissioners. Buntemeyer continued as city manager, supervising seventeen city employees.

In the decade that lay ahead, the city's people would move from clearing land, draining marshes, and laying out and building roads to creating the institutions and activities that would make Coral Springs a home town. Ahead lay schools, churches, parks, a library, clubs, sports and, inevitably, the city's first municipal taxes. In this busy decade Coral Springs would emerge from its company-town beginning and function as an independent municipality.

But the transformation from wilderness to city would take some doing. As late as 1971 George Dorsey killed a sixty-four-inch rattlesnake in his yard in the Dells.

To get the decade started in appropriate fashion, the Broward County School Board in January 1970 passed a resolution for the construction of the city's first elementary school. One small seed was planted. In time it would blossom into one of South Florida's best school programs. By the end of the decade ten schools would be in operation.

The startup process, however, was not without its complications. At first, Coral Springs children had been bused to school in nearby Margate. A desegregation plan proposed in 1970 called for some of them to be bused to schools farther away, some of them predominantly black.

On August 10, 1970, the Women's Division of the Coral Springs Chamber of Commerce was formed specifically to fight the busing plan. The purpose was to generate as many letters as possible to be sent to Congressman Paul Rogers, protesting the action. Soon letters began pouring in not just from the tiny new town of Coral Springs but from southern Palm Beach County to Miami.

A target was set—fifty thousand letters by October 7, the first day of hearings in Washington. One day before departure the group was nearly seventeen thousand letters short, but nonetheless the goal was reached.

The first plan had been to mail the letters. When mailing costs were calculated, Commissioner Ed Heafy, whose wife Emily had been one of the founders of the women's group, concluded it would be easier, quicker, and more effective to carry them to Washington by plane. Joe Taravella authorized Coral Ridge Properties to purchase airline tickets for Heafy and three committee members, Mrs. Alice Varvoutis, Mrs. Charles Tisdale, and Mrs. Douglas Nolan, to take the fifty thousand letters to Congressman Rogers and the United States Supreme Court justices in person.

In November the U.S. Fifth Court of Appeals reversed existing policy and delayed the Broward school desegregation pairing and clustering order. By the time the plan was put into operation Coral Springs had a school of its own—and a core of concerned volunteers willing to work for its educational goals.

Horse country in Coral Springs was located just south of Wiles Road at Coral Hills Drive. The Saddle Club held horse shows in the early days of the town. Courtesy of Coral Ridge Properties

Apparently pleased with the progress Coral Springs was making, Westinghouse opened its new Electra Center, featuring "Turned-on-Living" for the 1970s. The eight-thousand-square-foot, two-story building displayed state-of-the-art kitchen systems, synthetic bricks, innovative lighting, air conditioning, and security detection systems. Joe Taravella called it "a mini-version of a World's Fair Exhibit." On April 15, 1970, the Company brought its board of directors down to meet in the new building. Two years later Westinghouse held its annual stockholders' meeting at its manufacturing plant, drawing a crowd of thirteen hundred shareholders.

Another April event received less fanfare, but it established an important precedent that has since become a part of the Coral Springs way of doing things. From a larger parcel of land given by CRP to the county for a school, the school board released six acres to the townspeople for use as a park and recreational area. The Lions Club, under the chairmanship of John Nekich, with the assistance of Col. Ralph Gray, set about raising funds to build a baseball diamond. The colonel made the first contribution, seventy-eight dollars, for the development of Lions Park. It became the city's first Little League ball park.

This sequence proved to be a pattern in later years, with the company or city contributing land for parks, and private citizens and clubs contributing the funds and manpoweer to develop them. Volunteerism and community involvement, later to be major forces in the life of Coral Springs, surfaced early.

The Coral Springs Volunteer Fire Deaprtment was

A familiar sight in early Coral Springs was the Marketeer, an experimental electric car built by Westinghouse. It was driven around town by Joe Taravella, president of Coral Ridge Properties. Courtesy of Coral Ridge Properties

The Women's Division of the Coral Springs Chamber of Commerce mounted a spirited campaign to produce letters to Congress, protesting a busing order in 1970. The result was an outpouring of fifty thousand letters. Preparing them for air shipment to Congressman Paul Rogers were, left to right, Marian Nolan, Betty Larsen, Helene Sullivan and Jan Singer. Courtesy of Ed and Emily Heafy

On June 6, 1970, Lions Park was dedicated with some stout-hearted batting practice. It would become the city's first Little League ball park. Courtesy of Coral Ridge Properties

*The winner of the Coral Springs Open was not Arnold Palmer, the crowd's favorite, but a little-known Texan named Bill Garrett. In winning for the first time on the tour the gangling Texan took home a check for twenty-five thousand dollars for a 12-under-par 272. Trailing him were Bob Murphy, Vil Loustalot, Lee Trevino, Julius Boros and, in fifth place, Palmer.
Courtesy of Coral Ridge Properties*

incorporated in 1970. Founding members were Bob Fuller, the first fire chief, Russ Cagle, Bonnie Bonbrest, Raul Gosselin, Berry Ray, King Ducharme and city commissioner Ed Heafy. The department's first 750-gallon pumper truck was donated by CRP. Later the city would fund the cost of fire stations, equipment and operating expenses, but dedicated volunteers would continue to man the trucks and fight the fires.

The growing importance of the city was illustrated when Sample Road, which started at Federal Highway in Lighthouse Point, was extended into Coral Springs. The road, which would eventually reach all the way to the Flood Control District levee, provided a scenic drive through farmland and wooded areas to "the city in the country," a phrase later used by CRP in its advertising copy.

The May 27 dedication of Sample Road was marked not by a classic ribbon-cutting but by a "ribbon-crashing." Taravella and Mayor MacGregor drove through a ribbon in the Marketeer, an experimental, all-electric, fumeless automobile built by Westinghouse.

For the first time the city faced the possibility of having to levy a municipal property tax. The city's 1970-1971 budget of $292,000 projected a deficit of $148,320 plus $50,000 for planned capital improvements. The threat of taxes vanished when Coral Ridge Properties covered the city deficit. It was not until 1974 that an independent city government had to levy its first taxes.

In October ground was broken for the First Presbyterian Church at the intersection of Royal Palm Boulevard and Riverside Drive. It was scheduled for completion in the winter of 1971. Meanwhile other religious groups, particularly members of the Catholic and Methodist faiths, were beginning to hold meetings at various locations in the city.

As 1970 drew to a close the city stepped into the spotlight when the $125,000 Coral Springs Open Golf Tournament was held at the new Coral Springs Country Club golf course. Media coverage of the PGA-sanctioned tournament flashed the unfamiliar dateline "Coral Springs" all over the country. Texan Bill Garrett won the $25,000 first prize with his first victory on the PGA tour.

Not every enterprise in the growing city of Coral Springs prospered. The year after the tournament, the country club ran into problems. Coral Ridge Properties had to take the bankrupt club back from the operators who had leased it. It was reopened under new management as the Coral Springs Golf and Tennis Club.

For years Robert L. Hofmann, senior vice-president at CRP, had cultivated the friendship of Luther S. Remsburg. He hoped one day the company would be able to buy the Remsburg ranch just north of Wiles Road. One day Remsburg told him he was ready to sell. After a half century in Broward he decided it was time to move away from the fast-growing city adjoining his ranch and on to the less "citified" world of Okeechobee County. With Luther Remsburg, Hofmann later recalled, "a handshake was good enough." Coral Ridge Properties paid him $9 million for three thousand acres. The purchase price reflected the sharp increase in land values in the area in less than a decade. The first Lena Lyons land had been bought for $259 an acre; the Remsburg tract brought $3,000 an acre.

The Remsburg purchase in 1971 increased the size of the city to 13,400 acres. Taravella called it "the largest tract under master planning in South Florida's lower East Coast." Under the CRP "phased village concept" 49.3 percent of the land was devoted to open space—parks, lakes, streams, canals and public facilities. In response to the city's rapid growth, $7 million had been expended for a new sewer plant for the western areas and for the tripling of the capacity of the water-sewer system for the original acreage. Nearly $4 million had been allocated for extensive drainage and earth-moving projects for the city's southern area.

That summer Russell Rowe was named principal of the Coral Springs Elementary School. At first the school consisted of portable buildings, and not enough of them at that. A fast-growing city of young families swelled an anticipated enrollment of 350 students to an actual 550 and forced double sessions at the twelve portables.

An organization that would prove vital to the quality of education in Coral Springs was established in 1971. Charter officers for the Coral Springs Parent-Teacher Organization were Paul Singer, president; Jeannie Smith, vice-president, and Irvin Newberry, treasurer.

Westinghouse's Electra Lab home achieved a bit of unexpected fame in 1970 when golf pro Arnold Palmer stayed in the model when he played in the Coral Springs Open. A sign at the house announced, "Arnie Palmer slept here." Courtesy of Coral Ridge Properties

The Electra football team works out on the Sample Road practice field. Courtesy of Coral Ridge Properties

By 1971 the police department had grown from one officer and one dog to five officers with three patrol cars. Courtesy of Coral Ridge Properties

Principal Russell Rowe speaks at the dedication of Coral Springs' first school, the James S. Hunt Elementary School, in 1972. Courtesy of Coral Ridge Properties

In 1971 a highly independent newspaper made its appearance in Coral Springs. Observing that the Chamber of Commerce's *Coral Springs Chronicle* was little more than a sales sheet for Coral Ridge Properties, the Coral Springs Teen Association started the *Forum,* an independent, mimeographed publication. On September 18, 1971, Suzanne McElderry took the school board to task for delays in school construction; her story was headlined, "Promises, Promises." The paper's fire department reporter used the by-line Red Flame. Its future sports editor was Scoop, actually a ringer named Ed Heafy, a sports fan of boundless enthusiasm.

In time the *Forum* suspended publication, but the club had the good sense to sell the name. Consequently, still publishing in Coral Springs is the *Forum,* along with another weekly, the *Coral Springs News,* and a magazine named *Coral Springs Monthly.*

In December of 1971 ground was broken for a twenty-acre park to serve many community interests, baseball, tennis, swimming. The development of the park was enthusiastically supported by many community organizations, among them the Women's Club, the Lions Club, the Welcome Wagon Club and the Civic Association. It would become Mullins Park, named for Coral Springs, first elected mayor.

When the year ended, citizens of Coral Springs could look back on 1971 as a year of "firsts": first organized baseball, football, and basketball leagues; first church building; first school; first library; first supermarket, and first shopping center, plus the establishment of such organizations as the Jaycees, the Elks, the PTO and the Touchdown Club.

Elected to the city commission on January 18, 1972, were two incumbent commissioners, Ed Heafy and James Edwards, and Walter Blake, named to a two-year term. Edwards was named mayor at the January 18 meeting of the commission. Heafy, a pipe-smoking Irishman from New Brunswick, New Jersey, who had moved from Fort Lauderdale to Broken Woods Estates in 1968, would go on to serve on the city commission for eighteen years. His tenure included three years as mayor. He won his first term on the city commission in 1970. After the regular ballots were counted, he trailed by one vote but won the election by sweeping all six absentee ballots.

In February James S. Hunt, the father of Coral Springs, died at age 74. The *Quad City News* called the Old Man "America's most honored developer." In July the Broward County School Board paid its tribute by renaming the city's first school, the James S. Hunt Elementary School. As a developer, Hunt had done his job so well that only a month later the school's enrollment of 862 students exceeded its design capacity by 200 pupils.

By 1972 the Jewish population of the city had grown sufficiently to warrant the organization of the Coral Springs Hebrew Congregation. Its first meeting was held on August 11 in the Westinghouse Home Center. Religious services were followed by a general organizational meeting.

In the summer of 1972 the city commission wrestled with a number of problems that concern any growing municipality. A resolution requested the federal government to establish a permanent post office. Since 1969 a contract station had been funded by Coral Ridge Properties at a cost of twenty-five thousand dollars a year. Other matters demanding the attention of the commission were the question of fluoridating city water, zoning for large apartment complexes, tougher dog control ordinances, and the acquisition of land for a municipal complex.

On September 5 the city commission officially assumed responsibility for the Coral Springs Library. It had been founded by the Welcome Wagon Club and supported by volunteers and many other groups. Appointed by the commission to the first library board were Virginia Brannock, Ralph Morgen, Carol Powell, Dorothy Reiss, and Marina Taylor.

The city's first bank, the Bank of Coral Springs, opened its doors on September 12, 1972, in the Village Square Shopping Center. Over two thousand people showed up for cider, doughnuts and door prizes and left behind $3 million in deposits. Ten-year-old Diane Gordon, the bank's youngest stockholder, made it official by cutting a ribbon of dollar bills. Named as president was Bob Hofmann, CRP senior vice-president; the first cashier was Draper H. Hodges.

In 1973 the worldwide shortage of oil sent prices soaring for petroleum products. Its impact was felt in Coral Springs not just at the gasoline pump but in the residential sales approach of Westinghouse. Since acquiring Coral Ridge Properties in 1966, Westinghouse had aggressively merchandized its Electra Home. The model featured the "Kitchen of the Future," complete with advanced appliances and, including a fast new way of cooking without generating heat—later popular as microwave. Remote switches in Electra Homes would turn on radios and television, switch channels, open and close draperies, open and close garage doors. A hundred thousand people a year flocked to Coral Springs to see the futuristic electronic world ahead. These homes attracted future home buyers who were encouraged to make maximum use of electricity. And why not? Electricity was cheap.

Then came OPEC. When the energy crisis hit,

In 1972 the city assumed responsibility for the Coral Springs Library, located in the Coral Ridge Properties Administration Building. Courtesy of Coral Ridge Properties

Moving day for the first building built in Coral Springs came in May 1972, when it was hauled from Wiles Roads and State Road 7 to the Park of Industry. Over the years it served as the first police station, a clubhouse for the Jaycees, and a home for the Coral Springs Historical Society. In 1977 it was turned over to the fire department, which used it for fire training. In 1978 it was rescued from smoke and flame by the Landmark Restoration Committee. It sits now in Mullins Park as the Mini-Museum. Courtesy of Coral Ridge Properties

The dedication of Mullins Park was an assured success after five-year-old Debbie Reynolds wielded the first shovel. Courtesy of Coral Ridge Properties

Wilfred Neale, Jr., makes a point at a commission meeting in the early 1970s. Present at the meeting were, counter-clockwise from the top, city manager Werner Buntemeyer, mayor James Edwards and commissioners Ed Heafy, Walter Blake, George MacGregor, Neale, attorney Paul McDonough, and secretary Virginia Sartory. Courtesy of Coral Ridge Properties

Westinghouse had to change its approach as the cost of oil drove up the cost of generating electricity. Westinghouse moved then to develop an energy-conservation home. A new Electra Home utilized solar panels to heat water and swimming pools.

In 1974 new faces appeared on the political scene. Janet MacGregor, wife of the city's fourth elected mayor, decided to have a try at politics herself. The operator of the city's first printing shop, Janet MacGregor ran successfully for the Broward County School Board, a remarkable achievement in light of the tiny political base from which she operated. As Coral Springs increased in population, she would be followed by others who would win county-wide office from Coral Springs—Pat Nicholson and Jan Cummings, county school board, and George Platt and Marcia Beach, county commission. In addition, Peter Weinstein would be elected to the State Senate and Joe Titone to the State House.

The same year Janet MacGregor was elected, a major political figure appeared on the local scene. He was O. Benjamin Geiger, a towering—six foot six—fourth-generation Floridian descended from Creek Indians. One of his ancestors was a famous Key West character named Captain Geiger, whose home is preserved today as the Audubon House.

Geiger was elected mayor on what he admits was a strange platform. "I promised to raise taxes, well, not really just to raise them, to start them. We went from no tax to 4 mils. We had to bite the bomb, not the bullet. We didn't like being subsidized. We had to establish our independence."

When astronaut Gordon Mitchell, with arms folded, visited Coral Springs, George Hodapp, of Coral Ridge Properties, showed him the Westinghouse Experimental Home of the Future, complete with solar heating panels. Mitchell, who had piloted a spaceship around the moon, could not get his rental car started in Coral Springs. Courtesy of Coral Ridge Properties

The city's Green Canopy Program, aimed at beautifying Coral Springs, got off to a good start when Congressman Paul Rogers, left, and Joe Taravella, CRP president, pitched in to plant the first tree, supported in their goal by Girl Scouts. Courtesy of Coral Ridge Properties

Coral Ridge Properties was just as anxious to break the connection, Geiger recalls:

"Joe Taravella said, 'You better know what business you're in.' He didn't want to run a city, he wanted to form one."

When Buntemeyer left his unpaid post with the city, the new city government tried to hire him as its first full-time city manager, paid by city funds. Buntemeyer preferred to stay on with Coral Ridge Properties, which he would later serve as its president.

For its first full-time city manager the city selected Phillip R. Kelley, who had run the city government in Pascagoula, Mississippi. He held the Coral Springs position from January of 1974 until July of 1978.

One task that lay ahead for attorney Paul McDonough was the codification of various CRP procedures and restrictions into city ordinances and the modification of the 1963 charter into a document more closely tuned to governing the changing city. For instance, he eliminated sections relating to wharves, train whistles, and slaughterhouses, which had been carried over from the original charter quickly assembled from the Fort Lauderdale charter.

An important part of the new city charter established a strong city manager form of government. The commissioners were determined that the city would be run by professionals and the role of elected officials would be limited to setting policy.

"We wanted citizen-commissioners," said Ben Geiger. "Neither the mayor nor the commissioners have offices here. We don't even have parking places."

While McDonough was wrestling with the city's laws, Jerry Mucci, planning director for the city, was working to convert the CRP Master Plan into the city's blueprint for the future. Heavy emphasis on planning was the practice from the earliest days. Don Eveker, a volunteer fireman who later became the city's first administrator, recalls the ideas that went into the plans for the fire department.

"Headquarters was in a central location," he said, "and plans were made for four more stations, all of them located to avoid any crossing by emergency equipment on the way to a fire."

The year after the gasoline shortage hit, the nation faced a recession. Particularly hard hit were the Florida real estate and construction industries. Armed with ample funding and confidence that Florida would bounce back in short order, Taravella took an approach totally different from other developers. Instead of cutting back, he pushed ahead with the construction of two major high-rise buildings, the twelve-story Country Club Tower condominium on West Sample Road and the new ten-story Bank of Coral Springs Building. The bank building on the southwest corner of Sample Road and University Drive became the CRP's corporate headquarters.

When the company moved into its new offices in the fall of 1976, an important symbolic action became possible. The city had formerly leased office space on the second floor of the west buildings in Village Square Shopping Center. CRP offered to sell its Administration Building to the city. The company had constructed the building in 1966, complete with Old Virginia columns. East and west wings had been added in 1972.

In a late-night session in the winter of 1977 the commission voted to buy the building. The swiftness of the action drew criticism, but the commissioners' judgment proved to be sound. Appraised at $1.8 million, the building was purchased for $1.2 million. Annual payments were $99,500 plus 4.5 percent interest; the city's promissory note was signed by Mayor Heafy. The three-building complex contained nearly thirty-two thousand square feet. Its west wing served as the Coral Springs Library until 1982, when a new facility was built opposite Mullins Park. With municipal ownership of its own city hall, the city of Coral Springs had come of age.

Nova University, headquartered in Davie in South Broward County, established an educational unit in Coral Springs in 1976 to serve North Broward County and Palm Beach County. Undergraduate courses leading to the bachelor of science degree in a variety of majors thus became available in a city which was already actively developing a strong public school program.

The year 1978 produced a number of memorable developments. Coral Springs Mall, a $9.5 million enclosed and air-conditioned shopping center of semiregional size, opened its doors. The new mall, more than two hundred thousand square feet in size, provided more retail outlets for shoppers and roughly five hundred jobs to add to the growing employment opportunities. Meanwhile, Coral Ridge Properties moved ahead with plans for the city's first hotel, a 150-room Holiday Inn.

In August the Westinghouse Relay-Instrument Division, a business dating back to 1891, relocated from Newark, New Jersey, to the Park of Industry. The division sold the instrument product line in late 1984 and changed its name to Westinghouse Relay and Telecommunications Division. Within a decade the

In early 1975 Coral Springs was still a city with many open spaces. At right center is Financial Plaza, while homes and multifamilly dwellings arise elsewhere. Courtesy of Coral Ridge Properties

The city's first high school, Coral Springs High School, opened its doors for the 1975-1976 season. Courtesy of Coral Ridge Properties

In 1975 work was progressing on Briarwood 4. Briarwood was the city's first high-rise condominium. Courtesy of Coral Ridge Properties

A goal in the mid-seventies was raising $175,000 to build a stadium for Coral Springs High School. Members of the Coral Springs Kiwanis Club donated more than $600 to the stadium fund. Courtesy of Coral Ridge Properties

Little League Baseball opened on March 20, 1976, with city commissioner Jack Nordlund, at left, and CRP president Joe Taravella, in center behind two Little Leaguers. Courtesy of Coral Ridge Properties

division was providing some 350 jobs.

That same eventful year Helen G. Taché, a retiree from suburban Chicago who had formed the Property Owners Association, became the first woman ever elected to the city commission.

The year, however, also produced a sad development. On Thanksgiving Day, 1978, Joe Taravella, who had served as chief executive officer for Coral Ridge Properties for a dozen trail-blazing years, died of cancer. James Hunt, supersalesman, had supplied the dream, but it was Joe Taravella, the hard-driving chief executive officer, who had made Coral Springs work.

When the decade ended, the basic lines of the new city had been set. Major roads and canals had been built. Shopping centers were in operation, serving the retail needs of the residents; large office buildings had been constructed; the industrial park was under way. Residents had approved of bond issues for a new library building, a public safety building and new fire stations.

During the decade a city conceived as a retirement village became the home instead of young, growing families. So many children were living in Coral Springs that no less than ten public schools had to be added in the decade. Involvement by parents in those schools helped create a pressure for quality education that became the principal magnet that continues to pull more and more young families into Coral Springs.

As the Coral Springs High School Colts football team made ready for the 1976 season, four staunch supporters gathered to cheer them on. Left to right are Al Hugins, Coral Ridge Properties, Paul Profitt, school principal, Jim Caldwell, athletic director, and Chuck Connor, Coral Ridge Properties. Courtesy of Coral Ridge Properties

In the election year of 1976 President Gerald Ford visited Coral Springs. He told Coral Springs High School baseball players he would return, and return he did to visit the school and later to play in a pro-am golf tournament at Eagle Trace. Courtesy of Coral Ridge Properties

In the election year of 1976 Ronald Reagan also campaigned in Coral Springs. To his right sits Ben Geiger, who was a commissioner at that time. Courtesy of Coral Ridge Properties

When Broward County's first professional soccer team, the Fort Lauderdale Strikers, began play in 1977, the city of Coral Springs proved to be its strongest supporter. Welcoming the North American Soccer League team were, left to right, vice-mayor Carl Zeytoonian; commissioners Helen Taché and Ben Geiger; Elizabeth Robbie, the team's owner; coach Ron Newman; and mayor Ed Heafy. Photo by Kenneth Twaddell; courtesy of Ed and Emily Heafy

The 1977 dedication of the Ramblewood Fire Station drew a varied crowd to the stage. Jennifer Abrams, daughter of Richard Abrams, one of the department's chiefs, carried a strong endorsement of firemen on her T-shirt and also brought along the department's friendly Dalmatian, the official dog of fire departments everywhere. Standing beside Jennifer was Congressman Paul Rogers. Seated left to right were mayor Ed Heafy, city manager Phil Kelley, commissioner Jack Nordlund, Bob Hofmann, soon to become president of Coral Ridge Properties, and Chief Abrams. Courtesy of Coral Ridge Properties

A look north on University Drive in 1977 reveals only a few buildings, First Federal of Broward and Financial Plaza on the left and the high-rise towers of Briarwood on the right. Courtesy of Coral Ridge Properties

In the winter of 1977 the city of Coral Springs purchased the Coral Ridge Properties Administration Building, which is today City Hall. Mayor Ed Heafy hands the first payment to Bob Hofmann, chief financial officer at CRP. At rear, left to right, are city commissioner Ben Geiger, attorney Paul McDonough, city clerk Jonda Joseph, and city manager Phillip Kelley. Courtesy of Ed and Emily Heafy

Mayor Ed Heafy beams, understandably, as he presents the key to the city to Miss Florida at a Founders Day luncheon on April 30, 1977. Miss Florida that year was Nancy Stafford, from nearby Wilton Manors, a local favorite who would go on to star in television commercials and such dramas as St. Elsewhere and Matlock. Courtesy of Ed and Emily Heafy

In August 1978, the Westinghouse Relay-Instrument Division, which dated back to 1891, relocated from Newark, New Jersey, to Coral Springs. Courtesy of Westinghouse Relay and Telecommunications Division

In 1978 the Coral Springs Mall, under construction in this photograph, opened its doors. The $9.5-million shopping center contained more than two hundred thousand square feet and offered many new retail outlets to the growing city. Courtesy of Coral Ridge Properties

Enthusiastic Electra cheerleaders practice for the 1978 Our Town festival. Courtesy of Coral Ridge Properties

By the late 1970s the city of Coral Springs was taking shape. In the center the Financial Plaza had been completed and, just to the right, was the new Coral Springs Mall. At left center is Holiday Inn, the city's first hotel. Courtesy of Coral Ridge Properties

The $125,000 Coral Springs Open Golf Tournament at the new Coral Springs Country Club course drew some thirty thousand people for the week ending December 6, 1970. Many flocked to the course to see their favorite, Arnold Palmer, compete in the largest major sporting event ever held in Broward County up to that time. Media coverage of the Open put the city on the map nationally for the first time. Courtesy of Coral Ridge Properties

An eastward look on Sample Road still shows little traffic as late as 1982. Courtesy of Coral Ridge Properties

CHAPTER 4
THE EXPLODING EIGHTIES

In Florida population growth is generally regarded as a city or a county's ultimate measure of success. Broward County, the state's second most populous, was particularly proud when the census of 1980 showed it had officially reached the lofty goal of one million residents. Contributing heavily to the county's overall growth in the seventies had been the booming of Coral Springs. With a total of 37,349 residents Coral Springs had become the fastest growing city in the fastest growing county in the fastest growing state. Yet the steady increases of the 1970s were soon outdone by the explosive growth of the 1980s.

In 1983 the population hurtled past fifty thousand and in another two years had moved past sixty thousand. In 1987 it reached seventy thousand. By the time the city reached its twenty-fifth anniversary, its population approximated seventy-five thousand, and it had probably become the county's third largest city behind such older municipalities as Fort Lauderdale and Hollywood.

"The most important issues now are staying on top of growth and staying on top of schools," said Don Sanders, first elected to the Coral Springs city commission in 1980. He had come to the city in 1976 after visiting Fort Lauderdale earlier on spring break from Alfred University.

Jim Gordon, elected for the first time in 1983, had a similar observation: "Growth is both good and bad. It gives us an increased tax base, which means we can provide more services. It also means more traffic, more congestion. It means we have to have a larger police force. It now costs more to keep the city safe. That's the price you have to pay.

"Basically growth has been good for the city because it was planned. In general, the unprecedented growth we have seen has impacted the city in a positive manner."

A major change, Commissioner Gordon thinks, has been the shift of power away from the developer to the citizenry.

"It started with a great vision but it's wise to keep in mind that division between developer and citizens is necessary. Now the developer is going along one road, the citizens along another. The change is from the developer as the sole source of authority to turning it over to the people.

"The early planning showed entrepreneurial guts and vision. It set the stage we now play on and it gave us a pretty good map."

In November of 1980, Dodd A. Southern, who had been the assistant city manager, succeeded John A. Dow, Jr., as city manager. Dow, who had been the city's first director of parks and recreation, had also assumed the city managership after first serving as assistant to Phillip Kelley. Southern served until December of 1984. His assistant, Donald Sawyer, held the post of acting city manager briefly while the city commission decided that Coral Springs had now grown to the point where it needed the services of a city manager who had run cities of comparable size. William N. Brady, who had managed West Hartford, Connecticut, and Skokie, Illinois, became the Coral Springs city manager on March 19, 1985.

The Coral Springs Library moved into a new fifteen-thousand-square-foot structure on Northwest Twenty-ninth Street in the spring of 1982. The first city library had opened in May 1971, a project begun a year earlier by Welcome Wagon of Coral Springs. Welcome Wagon members canvassed door to door for donated books and held such fund-raising projects as square dances, auctions, raffles, fashion shows, and bridge and canasta parties. Coral Ridge Properties gave them space in the Teen Center in Village Square and the city donated shelves and office supplies and absorbed some of the startup costs. The first library had opened

In December 1982, high-speed chases, crashes and explosions were occurring in Coral Springs' "North 3,000" acres. The occasion was the filming of Smokey and the Bandit, Part 3. *Truck smashups were a feature of the film, and along the way a few members of the Ku Klux Klan ran into trouble. Courtesy of photographer Mark Freerks*

its doors with eleven hundred books. Two years later the library became a branch of the Broward County system; then in 1977 it moved into the west wing of City Hall. After the voters of Broward County passed a bond issue for library expansion in 1978, the library moved into its new quarters, where it now has approximately seventy-five thousand books.

That same year the city's retail scene received an enormous boost as plans moved ahead for the development of a regional shopping center equal in size to the county's largest, the Galleria in Fort Lauderdale. The project had been included in one of Coral Ridge Properties' earliest land plans. When H. J. Frazier, who had joined Westinghouse in 1973, became president of CRP's parent company, Community Development Group, he concluded that the time had come to fill in the designated area on the company's 1967 city plan.

Taravella had observed that many of the world's great shopping areas were basically strip shopping centers—Worth Avenue in Palm Beach, Rodeo Drive in Beverly Hills, Park Avenue in New York. He had concentrated on developing strip shopping centers along Sample Road, such as Village Green and Village Square. Frazier concluded the time had come for the city's first large regional shopping mall. He convinced the Edward J. DeBartolo Company, one of America's largest developers of shopping centers, to build Coral Square, a 1.2 million-square-foot enclosed mall at the intersection of University Drive and Atlantic Boulevard.

At the opening of the mall in October 1984, Frazier said: "Can you imagine the audacity of blocking out a regional mall here fifteen yeas ago?" He had a point. In 1967 fewer than five hundred people lived on a former cattle range. Now a mall had arisen, bringing to Coral Springs such major retailers as Burdines, Jordan Marsh, J. C. Penney, and Lord & Taylor's.

The long-range land plan for Coral Springs had

also called for a high-density area of multifamily dwellings in the southwestern area of the city. Said George Hodapp, who developed the master plan: "We liked the idea of high-rises looking out toward the Everglades at beautiful sunsets. The idea never caught on. We changed it to single-family, less density, less impact. That's the way the market wanted to move."

Frazier pushed ahead with the development of a two-square-mile portion of the southwestern planning area known originally as Village IX but presented to the buying public as Eagle Trace. In 1982 he had declared the new development would "be one of America's finest residential areas."

An integral element in the Eagle Trace complex was the creation of an eighteen-hole championship "stadium" golf course which would become a Tournament Players Club, owned and operated by the touring golf pros' organization.

The clubhouse built for TPC harked back to Jim Hunt's original dream of "a bit of Old Virginia." The two-story clubhouse, built on a knoll which towers some twenty-eight feet above sea level—and in south Florida twenty-eight feet is towering—is adapted from the design at the old plantation home, Carter's Grove, near Williamsburg.

The name of the golf-course architect chosen to design Eagle Trace proved to be prophetic. Art Hills, a famed architect from Toledo, Ohio, laid out a course with a rare feature for south Florida—hills. For years Coral Ridge Properties had been dumping a wide variety of construction debris in an area where it planned one day to build a course. Over a period of nearly two decades this debris had created the foundation for South Florida hills.

Eagle Trace's hillsides provide the "stadium" feature the TPC requires for its courses. Spectators standing on the slopes are afforded an excellent view of the pros battling the bunkers and water hazards of a tough 7,037-yard course.

In 1984 the first Honda Classic, sponsored by the American Honda Motor Company, Inc., moved a few miles north to Eagle Trace from Lauderhill, where its predecessor, the Jackie Gleason Inverrary Classic, had been played.

From its first tournament, March 1 to 4, 1984, the Honda Classic at Eagle Trace has produced spectacular results. Bruce Lietzke and Curtis Strange won the first two in playoffs. In the third, in 1986, a little-known pro named Kenny Knox, who had to play a qualifying round to earn a spot in the tournament, became the champion. The 1987 tournament was won by Mark Calcavecchia, of West Palm Beach, who had caddied in the 1986 tournament. The 1988 winner was Joey Sindelar, from nearby Boca Raton, with a 13-under-par score of 275, tying the record set in 1985 by Strange and Peter Jacobsen, who lost out in the playoffs. For his victory Sindelar received a check for $126,000, more than five times the amount paid to Bill Garrett, the winner of the 1970 Coral Springs Open and roughly 12 percent of the price of the first land purchased which started the city on its way.

A hundred thousand people attended the week-long 1988 Honda Classic, and millions more watched it on NBC Television. The Honda Classic illustrated again

Among the stars of Smokey and the Bandit *were composer-singer-actor Paul Williams (above) and Jackie Gleason. Floridian Burt Reynolds made a cameo appearance. Courtesy of photographer Mark Freerks*

In 1982 Coral Ridge Properties announced plans for Eagle Trace, a new luxury community, built around a championship golf course and anchored by a clubhouse adapted from the design of a Virginia great house called Carter's Grove. Just this side of the clubhouse is the ninth green. Courtesy of Coral Ridge Properties

the spirit of volunteerism which has developed in Coral Springs over the years. Eleven hundred people, including Mayor Ben Geiger and City Commissioner Don Sanders, volunteered to help with tasks that included crowd control, keeping score, hospitality, child care for the children of the touring pros, and picking up trash.

Among the great names of golf who have played in the Honda Classic at Eagle Trace are Jack Nicklaus, Ray Floyd, Tom Weiskopf, Tom Kite, Craig Stadler, Hale Irwin, and such international stars as Greg Norman, Seve Ballesteros, Sandy Lyle, Nick Faldo, and Bernhard Langer. President Gerald Ford participated in the 1984 pro-am.

In 1983 Coral Springs observed its twentieth anniversary. The city had started with just five residents; in its anniversary year it welcomed its fifty thousandth resident to the city and annexed an additional 1.4 square miles to Coral Springs. New construction that year was valued at over $100 million. The real estate valuation in the city of Coral Springs had increased to over $1 billion, an increase of 28 percent over the previous year and a staggering amount past the $1 million Hunt had paid Lena Lyons for the first Coral Springs purchase two decades earlier.

In 1984 construction activity continued at a record pace of $132.7 million, more than 21 percent above the previous year's impressive totals. Ground was broken for the $40-million Coral Springs Medical Center.

Work also proceeded on the city's largest office building. Officially named the Coral Springs Sunrise Towers, its builders quickly learned that their black-glass structure had acquired the nickname of "the Darth Vader Building."

In 1984 a South Florida banker named Thomas L. Grossjung observed that none of the banks serving Coral Springs was headquartered in the city. Joining him to organize a bank, "owned and operated by Coral Springs residents" as its ads would later say, were John Trout, William Sproule, E. A. Salzer, Itchko Ezratti, Stuart Schechter, and Bob Hofmann, who had been president of the city's first bank, later acquired by Miami-based Southeast Bank.

On February 8, 1985, National City Bank opened with Grossjung as president and chief executive officer, and Trout as chairman of the board. Within two years the bank, located on University Drive, had amassed total assets of more then $25 million.

By 1985 Coral Springs' steady population growth had reached sixty-five thousand, making it the fourth largest of Broward County's twenty-eight municipalities and the fifteenth largest city in the state. The most far-reaching event of the year occurred on November 5, 1985, when voters went to the polls and voted for a $16-million bond program which would expand, renovate, and improve parks and recreation, police and fire department facilities and services, and build a fifty-thousand-square-foot community center.

In preparing the bond referendum for voter approval, Moody's and Standard and Poor's bond rating agencies raised Coral Springs' bond rating substantially, Moody's from Baa to A-1, and Standard and Poor's from BBB+ to A+.

Mayor Ben Geiger is fond of telling an anecdote about one of the bond agency representatives. When asked what impressed him most about the city, he told the mayor: "I was amazed to see not only hoops left up on the basketball backboards, but the nets as well. In most cities, you wouldn't dare leave the nets out for fear they'd be stolen."

As the city moved ahead toward its twenty-fifth anniversary, work continued on parks, and city facilities as well as private-sector construction of residential, business, and health facilities. In March of 1987 the two-hundred-bed Coral Springs Medical Center, a general medical and surgical facility, opened its doors, thus adding an important new service for the residents of Coral Springs.

For nearly two decades politicians and planners in Broward County had discussed the construction of an expressway that would traverse the western and northern cities in Broward. In 1978 Coral Springs had fought back an attempt to build one along Wiles Road. In June of 1986 the Sawgrass Expressway, a toll road, opened. The road was built north of Coral Springs, between the city and Parkland, and on its southward bend it cruised south on the west side of town. When completed, it will connect the northern end of the county with Interstates 75 and 95. At that time, it will become a tremendous asset to the city, opening up new industrial opportunities to companies in the Park of Industry.

Observing that the city was well stocked with

In 1984 work was proceeding on the city's largest office building, a black-glass structure, formally known as Coral Springs Sunrise Towers but usually referred to as the "Darth Vader" Building. Later it became the Coral Savings Centre. Courtesy of Coral Ridge Properties

On October 3, 1984, the Coral Square Mall celebrated its grand opening. Coral Square was built by the Edward J. DeBartolo Company, one of the country's largest mall developers. A regional mall, Coral Square was one of Broward's largest two malls, with more than a million square feet of shopping space. Courtesy of City of Coral Springs

The Reverend Billy Graham is a frequent visitor to Coral Springs, where he visits his daughter, a resident. Courtesy of Coral Ridge Properties

financial institutions headquartered in other cities and states, a group of investors received government approval to open Coral Savings and Loan Association in Coral Springs on March 13, 1987. Since the thirteenth was a Friday, the prudent organizers opened the new institution on March 16, a Monday. With Peter Hardiman, an experienced banker who had lived in Coral Springs since 1974, as its president, Coral Savings moved into the "Darth Vader" Building and gave it a new name—the Coral Savings Centre. Within a year it had accumulated $19 million in assets.

In the winter of 1987 *Florida Parent Magazine* published an article picking the best cities in Broward and Palm Beach counties for raising families. Selected as the best in a two-county area was Coral Springs. Wrote Bernard McCormick: "Coral Springs is not only the foremost family town in South Florida, it ranks second in youthfulness in the entire country."

For James Hunt, whose first concept for Coral Springs was a retirement community, the city's youthfulness would have come as a surprise. Yet the figures show that 30.2 percent of the city's population consists of school-age children, from five to seventeen, a figure bettered only by East St. Louis, Illinois.

For the election of 1988, two long-time members of the city commission, Ed Heafy and Helen Taché, stepped down. The stage was set for the single largest change in the commission's composition since the city's early days. When the votes were counted, the change was a large one indeed. Jeanne Mills and Janet Oppenheimer won election, thus placing two activist women on the city commission for the first time in history, each of them many years younger than the commissioners they succeeded.

Perhaps the most important event of the twenty-fifth anniversary year occurred on February 16, 1988. That evening at a city commission meeting, the city of Coral Springs handed a check for $103,977 to Coral Ridge Properties to complete the ten-year purchase of city hall. The check was the final installment on a $995,000 promissory note signed by Ed Heafy, who was mayor in 1977. The purchase price had been $1.2 million.

Willard Beck, director of finance for the city, suggested a note-burning ceremony to city manager Bill Brady.

"Sounds like a good idea," said Brady. And whom did he pick to burn the mortgage? Ed Heafy, who was then sitting as a member of the commission.

"We thought Ed should have the pleasure of burning the note since he originally signed it," said Brady.

It was a fitting way for a "new" city to close out its first twenty-five years.

Players start early at the tennis clinic at Mullins Park. Courtesy of City of Coral Springs

Firemen from throughout Broward County battle it out at the annual Firematics Competition at the Cagle Station in the Coral Springs Park of Industry. Courtesy of City of Coral Springs

Competition is intense at the Coral Springs BMX track. Courtesy of City of Coral Springs

With a par on the first play-off hole, Curtis Strange defeated Peter Jacobsen to win the 1985 Honda Classic. Strange, who shot a record 275 for 72 holes, displays the winner's trophy but was probably much more delighted with his winner's check for ninety thousand dollars. Courtesy of City of Coral Springs

Sgt. Jim Hanrahan supervises target practice for police cadets undergoing training for the Coral Springs police department. Courtesy of City of Coral Springs

Coral Springs motorcycle policemen must undergo recurrent training, part of it at an obstacle course at Mullins Park. Courtesy of City of Coral Springs

Freezing weather is an infrequent visitor to Coral Springs. Still, on February 22, 1985, ice appeared on automobile windshields in the city. Courtesy of City of Coral Springs

Runners get off the mark in the annual thirty-kilometer race in the fall of 1987. Courtesy of City of Coral Springs

Keeping Florida canals clear of aquatic weeds is a tough job. Pride Promoters of the Dells work at clearing them out. Left to right are two hard-working volunteers, Carl Sosnowsky, of Pride Promoters, and Warren Gilbert, chief of police. Courtesy of City of Coral Springs

Australian Greg Norman won the 1987 Honda Classic "Shoot-out" in a star-studded international field of golfers. Courtesy of City of Coral Springs

To raise money for the Leukemia Society, Coral Springs residents responded to an enticing offer at the Celebrity Waiters Luncheon for Leukemia: contribute a hundred dollars and have a "friend" of your choice squashed in the face by a pie. Mayor Ben Geiger does the honors to an unidentifiable woman. Not long after this defilement, the mayor in turn received a pie in the face. Courtesy of City of Coral Springs

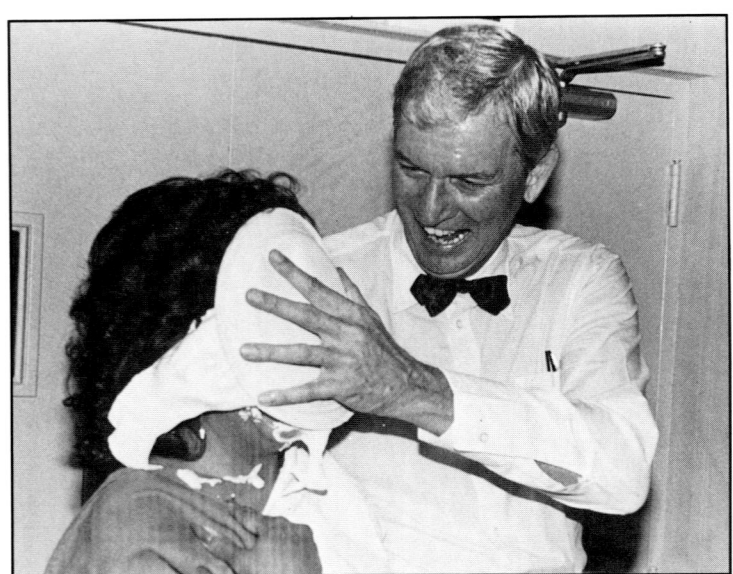

City commissioner Don Sanders and his wife Yvette compete in the annual ten-kilometer race. Courtesy of City of Coral Springs

The Annual Arts and Crafts Show is held each year at Financial Plaza. Courtesy of Coral Ridge Properties

During Fire Prevention Week the Coral Springs Fire Department's Fire Prevention Bureau visits city schools to discuss fire safety with students. Courtesy of City of Coral Springs

The Coral Springs Police Department takes particular pride in its marksmanship. Left to right are Lt. Randy Henderson, the "top gun" in Florida, Lt. Byron Stanley, Sgt. Gary Brown, and Sgt. Jim Hanrahan. Courtesy of City of Coral Springs

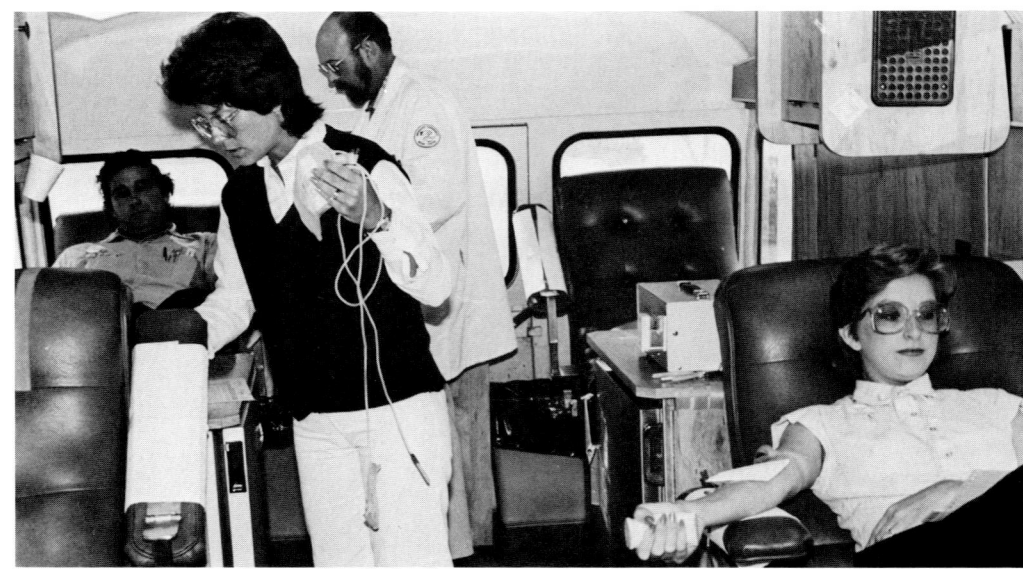

Sandi Gardner gives blood, one of many activities in which the Coral Springs spirit of volunteerism plays an important role. Courtesy of City of Coral Springs

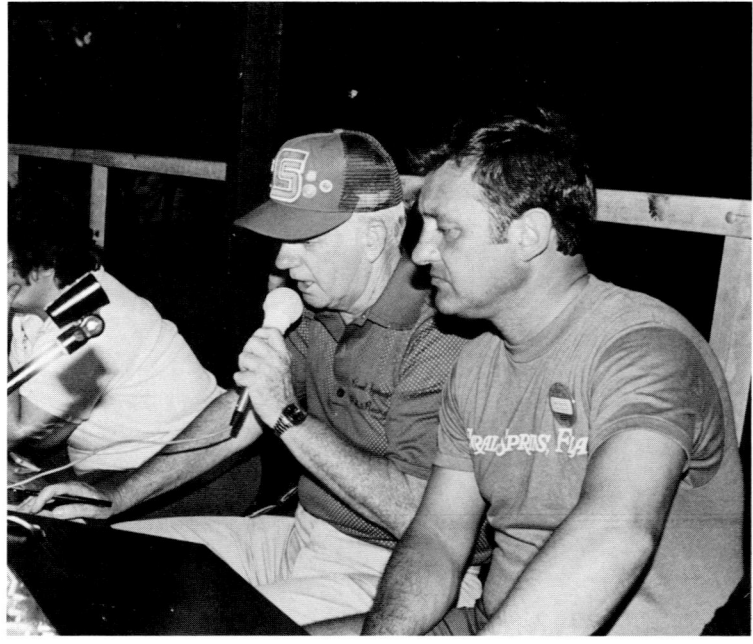

Sometimes the voice of sports is also the voice of the city commission. Two sportscasters of uncommon merit are Ed Heafy, left, and Don Sanders, shown here in action at the Southern Regional Baseball Tournament. They also handle the P.A. system at school and sandlot events. Courtesy of City of Coral Springs

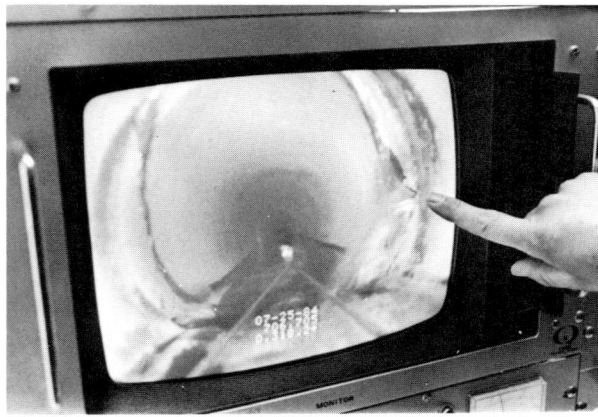

High-tech methods are brought into play to repair a leak in a Coral Springs water pipe. Closed-circuit television helps locate the site of the leak, thus enabling city crews to complete the repair. Courtesy of City of Coral Springs

Commissioner Don Sanders gained nationwide exposure when his outfit for the annual Celebrity Waiters Luncheon for leukemia was picked as the event's national logo.

Morrison's Cafeteria is well known in Florida as a purveyor of food. In Coral Springs the cafeteria was sold to the city and promptly converted into a supplementary office building. Courtesy of City of Coral Springs

Coral Springs children bury a time capsule at Mullins Park. The capsule, buried after the Challenger disaster, contains letters commemorating the astronauts and giving the children's views of the tragic event. Courtesy of City of Coral Springs

Judges at the annual Chili Country Cookoff at Mullins Park in 1986 sample a few scorching entries. The winner was Emily Heafy. Courtesy of City of Coral Springs

Dancers pep things up at the annual Chili Country Cookoff at Mullins Park. Courtesy of City of Coral Springs

Building inspectors, left to right, Bob Holtsclaw, chief inspector, and Lou Siano, check out construction at Eagle Trace. During 1987 inspections were carried out prior to the issuance of a certificate of occupancy for about a thousand residential units. Courtesy of City of Coral Springs

Work proceeds on the two-hundred-bed Coral Springs Medical Center, which opened in 1987. The center specializes in family-centered health care, including a twenty-four-bed maternity suite, a sixteen-bed pediatric pavilion and sixteen critical-care beds, six of them for neonatal intensive care. Courtesy of City of Coral Springs

Firemen place Christmas decorations on the Norfolk Island pine planted by Boy Scouts in 1970 on what was then Coral Ridge Properties land. Courtesy of City of Coral Springs

Coral Springs residents gather for the annual lighting of the Christmas tree at City Hall. Courtesy of City of Coral Springs

Police chief Warren Gilbert conducts a tour, showing citizens the new dispatch center at police headquarters. Courtesy of City of Coral Springs

The fire department's Fire Prevention Robot is interviewed by Don Eveker, administrator, while Jennifer Heafy operates a video camera for the "Forum Cable News." Courtesy of City of Coral Springs

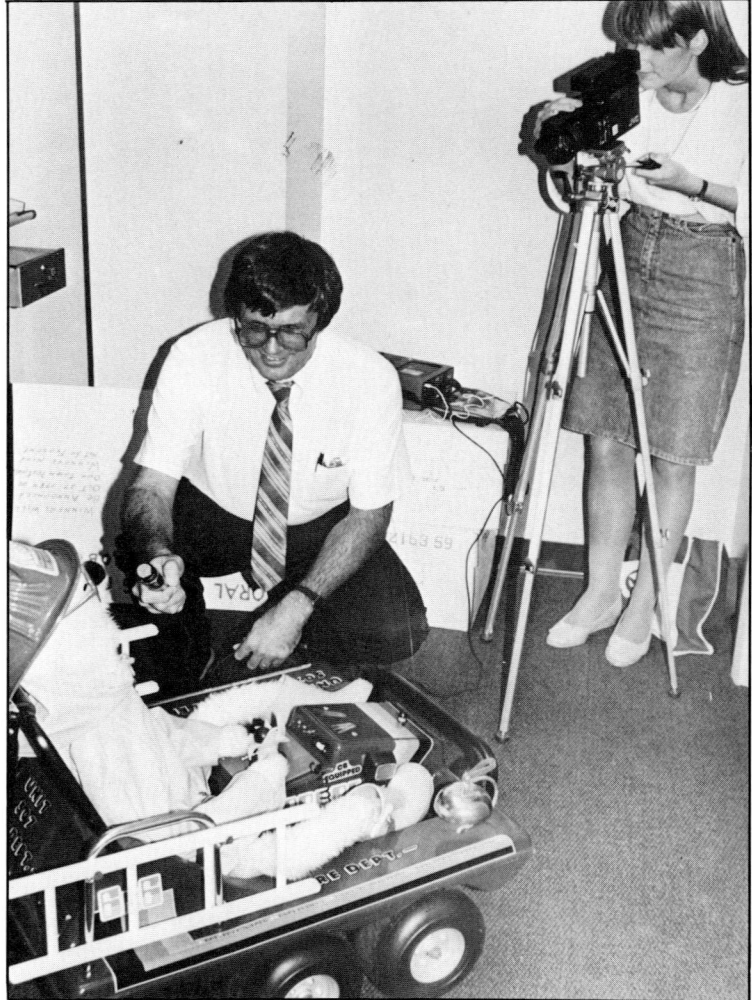

Coral Springs Police Color Guard marches in the Coral Springs Our Town parade. Courtesy of City of Coral Springs

Although most of the dwellings in Coral Springs are owner-occupied, nearly seven thousand multifamily rental units have been built in the 1980s. Over fifteen hundred new rentals were added in 1987. Courtesy of City of Coral Springs

The Coral Springs Medical Center, upper right center, opened in 1987 with two hundred beds, offering acute care and specializing in family-centered health care. Courtesy of City of Coral Springs

City employees operate a booth at the annual Fourth of July Picnic at Mullins Park. Courtesy of City of Coral Springs

The Coral Springs Summer Antics program gives kids supervised play at school playgrounds during the summer when school is out. Courtesy of City of Coral Springs

Mullins Park's fifty acres offer an enormous range of recreational activities for Coral Springs residents, including soccer, baseball, softball, T-ball, basketball, shuffleboard, horseshoes, a BMX track, a children's playground and a volleyball area. Courtesy of City of Coral Springs

Volleyball players battle it out at Mullins Park. Courtesy of City of Coral Springs

City horticulturist Carol Ingold works with kids, teaching them the art of beautifying Coral Springs through landscaping. Courtesy of City of Coral Springs

A young lady sizes up events at the annual Our Town festival. Courtesy of City of Coral Springs

By the mid-1980s the Westinghouse Relay and Telecommunications Division was employing roughly 350 people, which was fortunate since the Burroughs Corporation, which provided 500 jobs, closed in 1985 due to a company-wide consolidation. Courtesy of Coral Ridge Properties

Coral Springs kids eagerly greet Santa Claus. Courtesy of City of Coral Springs

Intercity baseball competition between the police and parks and recreation departments is intense at Mullins Park. Courtesy of City of Coral Springs

Since 1985 Coral Springs has played host to an unusual event, the annual Coral Springs Ashley Whippet Invitational. The invitational is a competition open to both novice and experienced frisbee-catching dogs who are judged on showmanship, catching, leaping ability, and degree of difficulty of the throws and catches. Courtesy of City of Coral Springs

Linda Facterman is a baseball fan; the shirt proves it. Her two sons play in the Coral Springs American Little League. The baseball shirts were offered for sale at the Our Town festival. Courtesy of City of Coral Springs

City commissioners and members of the Junior Chamber of Commerce break ground for a new Jaycee Park. Courtesy of City of Coral Springs

Responding to Coral Springs' enthusiasm for soccer, a number of international soccer stars have made their homes in the city, among them the famed Peruvian, Teofilo (Nene) Cubillas. Others include David Chadwick and the late Colin Fowles. Courtesy of City of Coral Springs

Firefighters battle a spectacular nighttime blaze on Coral Ridge Drive. Eighty-six volunteers fight Coral Springs fires; paid employees include only three in administration and five in fire inspection. Courtesy of City of Coral Springs

The election of 1988 brought two new faces to the Coral Springs City Commission—Jeanne Mills, left, and Janet Oppenheimer. Courtesy of City of Coral Springs

Paying off the mortgage is a great moment for anyone. Burning the promissory note for City Hall is an experience that brings smiles to, left to right, George Hodapp, vice-president, Coral Ridge Properties, the company which held the note; Jim Gordon, commissioner; Dan Groh, fire chief, holding a fire extinguisher, in case the flames in the hub cap get out of hand; and Commissioners Ed Heafy, Helen Taché, and Don Sanders. Courtesy of City of Coral Springs

Twenty-five years after the city was founded, the Covered Bridge has firmly established itself as the symbol of the city of Coral Springs. Courtesy of Coral Ridge Properties

CHAPTER 5
TWENTY-FIVE AND COUNTING

A drive along the northwest curve of the Sawgrass Expressway reveals Coral Springs as it was in 1963—ranchland, cattle grazing, no houses in sight. A turn off the Sawgrass onto New Sample Boulevard soon displays the city as it is twenty-five years later, almost as though the whole history of Coral Springs could be compressed into a short ten-minute drive.

Continue east on New Sample past the Park of Industry, the Country Club of Coral Springs, single-family homes, Country Club Tower, shopping centers, and, at the intersection of Sample Road and University Boulevard, the closest thing the city has to a downtown. Near the intersection are the city's largest two office buildings, Financial Plaza and Coral Savings Centre; the Coral Springs Mall; Holiday Inn; City Hall and the Gulf station, still conforming to Jim Hunt's dream of Old Virginia.

It is a busy intersection the year round. Since the city does not depend on tourism, as do so many Florida towns, Coral Springs remains a bustling city throughout all twelve months.

In its development the city has not depended on the classic force of transportation for its remarkable growth. Most cities grow out of some combination of transportation strengths—location on a harbor, a river, a railroad, or a highway, or near a major airport. Coral Springs has neither a port nor a railroad, despite references to them in its original charter. No major highway runs through the city and Coral Springs has no plans for even a small executive airport, although small planes landed on Sample Road in earlier times.

Without the aid of tourism or transportation the city has nonetheless moved briskly ahead. From five lonely residents, Coral Springs has grown to a city of seventy-five thousand residents in just a quarter of a century. The city will probably be Broward's third largest by the census of 1990, if not before then, although every city in the county, with one exception, is older.

What, then, has fueled the town's growth? For the first quarter of a century the moving force in building Coral Springs has been just that—the job of building Coral Springs. Building permits for 1987 totaled more than $125 million. As the town has grown, it has generated the need for more services and thus has created more employment. The first settlers all had jobs in Coral Springs; after all, they worked for the developer. By 1988 the number of jobs within the city had risen to more than twenty-two thousand.

How much more will Coral Springs grow? Dennis Foltz, city planning director, estimates the population will total roughly 150,000 by buildout in 2010, but admits his figures may be high. Despite provisions for high-density areas, the city has tended to grow in a low-density pattern which in turn has made it a comfortable home town for families.

Although Hunt had conceived the city as a retirement community, it soon moved in the opposite direction. According to the latest census figures, more than a third of its population is in the twenty-five to forty-four age bracket. Eighty-eight percent of the households are families, and the size of the families, 3.27 people per household, is the largest in Florida and tied for first place in the Southeast. Its population of school-age children, five to seventeen, is the second highest in the nation.

Furthermore, Coral Springs families are well equipped to care for their children. The median household income in Coral Springs is $40,654, the highest in the southeastern states; average income is even higher, $47,344.

Warren Gilbert, who has served the city across nearly two-thirds of its existence, reports that Coral Springs has the lowest major crime rate of all cities of comparable size and population in Florida. The city,

The Joseph P. Taravella High School, named after the late president of Coral Ridge Properties, opened in 1981. Courtesy of City of Coral Springs

At Ramblewood Middle School children attend an informal Youth Liaison Program session conducted by the Coral Springs police department. In every school in the city, uniformed police conduct safety, law-enforcement, and drug-and-alcohol-abuse programs and provide counseling. Courtesy of City of Coral Springs

Phil Murch presents the Coral Springs High School girls' basketball team to the city commission at the start of a drive to raise funds to send the team to a Seattle tournament. The funding drive was successful. Courtesy of City of Coral Springs

Mary Rogers, formerly of the city of Coral Springs personnel department, speaks to elementary school children about careers in city government during Career Day. Courtesy of City of Coral Springs

however, has not been spared the problems associated with a youthful and affluent population. Uniformed youth liaison officers, stationed in Coral Springs schools since 1976, present drug and alcohol abuse programs to students, along with youth counseling and bicycle safety competitions.

"The department is heavily involved in education," says Chief Gilbert, "and the city provides resources for our programs."

The quality of Coral Springs schools offers the best explanation for the city's attraction for young families. Coral Springs is served by thirty schools, thirteen of them a part of the Broward public school system, the eighth largest in the nation. Sol Aboulafia, former Broward "Teacher of the Year" and now research director for Coral Ridge Properties, has tried to pin down the reasons for the schools' success.

"What distinguishes public schools in Coral Springs from other counterparts in some other county areas," he said, "is the combination of active supportive administration at each school, large numbers of parents assisting with myriads of school projects, enthusiastic, dynamic and dedicated instructors, well-behaved, well-disciplined, and cooperative students and a binding sense of unity and pride within the City of Coral Springs."

Jeanne Mills, newly elected city commissioner, has been active in the schools since she, her husband and their three boys arrived in Coral Springs a dozen years ago. She is a former president of the Broward County Parent-Teacher Association as well as a long-time member of school and district advisory committees. In trying to explain the success of the schools in Coral Springs, she said: "We have a unique situation here, unlike any other in the county. We have the largest volunteer group in the county, not just parents but senior citizens too. Not just kids, we have parents, too."

Scholastic awards won by Coral Springs students include Westinghouse Science Talent Search honors and Governor's Pride Award in math. Teachers have won the Presidential Award in Chemistry and state teacher awards in biology, earth science, the gifted program, and home economics. More than 86 percent of the city's students graduate, a figure exceeded in the southeastern states only by the university town of Chapel Hill, North Carolina.

Former city manager William Brady, who came to Coral Springs after managing two affluent cities of comparable size, has observed that the socio-economic basics were similar to those in his former locations, West Hartford and Skokie, but one difference he found quite striking.

"There's a strong feeling here about youth, education and recreation," he said. "The unusual character in this is the volunteerism. You have twelve thousand volunteers in the city, primarily in recreation and the fire service. This means we have a very low ratio of staff to the number and variety of events. There is so much here the city doesn't have to pay for. We help groups who want to get an activity started, but no cash handouts."

Arriving in Coral Springs a decade after CRP's Werner Buntemeyer had stepped down as the first city

Children at Maplewood Elementary School release balloons bearing the anti-drug message "Just Say No." The balloons were carried by the wind over most of Broward County. Courtesy of City of Coral Springs

manager, Brady observed that the days when the city was a company town are "long gone." As an example of the independence that now exists between the city and company, he commented: "We've brought lawsuits against them and they've sued us."

In its early stages Coral Springs was clearly a developer town. "We had to subsidize everything because no one wanted to build out here," Gordon Ickes told Flynn McRoberts, a *Miami Herald* reporter. "In the old days it was a real company town. In recent years the government and the company have taken separate paths. The people are now firmly in control of the government."

Coral Ridge Properties, Ickes said, wanted to avoid the label of "company town." He feels now that CRP has been successful—maybe too successful. A recent company survey showed that nine of ten Coral Springs residents had never heard of Coral Ridge Properties. "We're doing one helluva PR job," he said.

From the beginning the company tried to minimize the role of politics in city government by keeping personalities out of the picture.

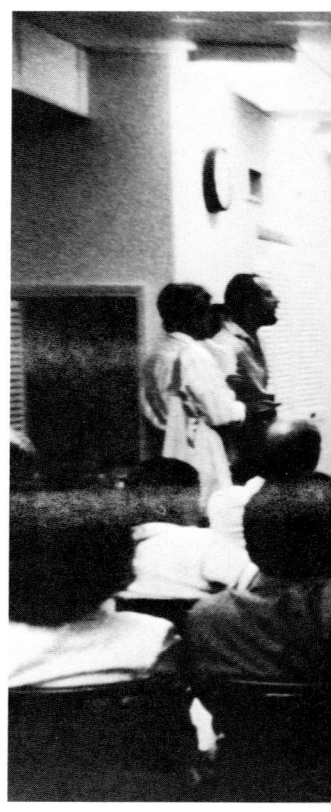

School volunteers are honored at a luncheon at the Holiday Inn in April of 1987. Over twelve thousand residents are active as volunteers in Coral Springs. Courtesy of City of Coral Springs

City commission meetings in Coral Springs regularly draw large crowds of citizens. Presiding at this meeting is Mayor Ben Geiger, center; at far right is City Manager William Brady. Courtesy of City of Coral Springs

The city has been basically scandal-free; elections and city commission meetings have been relatively clear of issues and controversies. Commissioners often run for reelection without opposition, a sign incumbents believe means that citizens are reasonably satisfied with the city government. "We don't have down-and-dirty council meetings," observed Jeanne Mills.

Some have called Coral Springs "yuppie heaven," others a "designer" city. On June 8, 1986, Carol Weber, associate publisher of the *Miami Herald*'s Broward edition, wrote:

"OK, they have to admit it, there is a certain Disney World feel to Coral Springs... This is basically a conservative, White Anglo-Saxon Protestant sort of a place filled with polite Chamber of Commerce members. You get the feeling that if someone in a passing car were to throw litter out the window, some smiling uniformed person would dart out of a nearby doorway with a broom and one of those long-handled dust pans and quickly shovel it out of sight, into tombs under the streets.

"But it works. The city works."

CHAPTER 6
CORAL SPRINGS TODAY

The major industry throughout Coral Springs' first twenty-five years has been construction, the building of the city itself. Courtesy of Coral Ridge Properties

Participants assemble in the staging area for the 1986 Our Town parade. Courtesy of City of Coral Springs

In 1968 the Coral Ridge Properties' Administration Building was one of the few structures in the city. Courtesy of Coral Ridge Properties

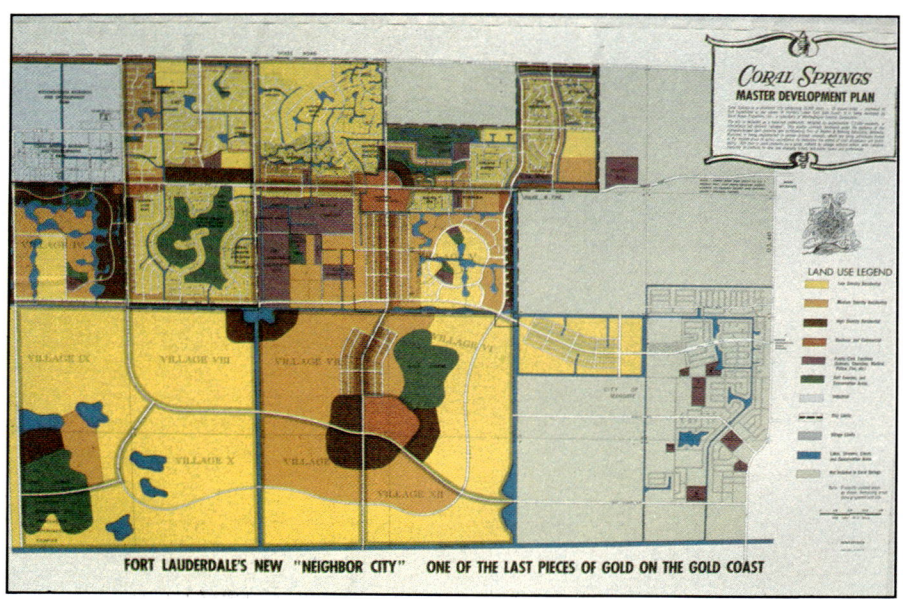

The master plan for Coral Springs was beginning to take shape as early as the mid-1960s. Courtesy of Coral Ridge Properties

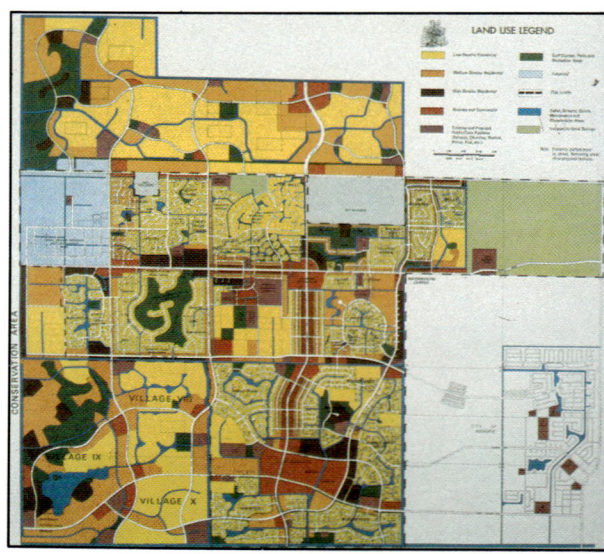

By the 1980s much of the Coral Springs master plan had been fulfilled. Courtesy of City of Coral Springs

The Senior League Baseball Southern Regional Tournament is always a premier event in the baseball-happy city of Coral Springs. Courtesy of City of Coral Springs

In 1986 a baseball fan pays tribute to the home team in the Southern Regional Tournament. Courtesy of City of Coral Springs

Water polo is a hotly contested sport at the Mullins Park pool. Courtesy of City of Coral Springs

Coral Springs soccer teams battle it out for the McGuire Cup. Courtesy of City of Coral Springs

The Mullins Park pool draws a crowd when the South Florida weather heats up. Courtesy of City of Coral Springs

BMX racers provide a colorful display at Mullins Park. Courtesy of City of Coral Springs

Basketball courts are kept in prime condition for the city's players. Courtesy of City of Coral Springs

An aerial view reveals the playing fields of Mullins Park. Courtesy of City of Coral Springs

Beautifully decorated at Christmas is the home of Mario Ruffalo, a Sample Road hardware merchant whose impact has been large in Coral Springs. Courtesy of City of Coral Springs

Blind golfers compete in a tournament at the Country Club of Coral Springs. Courtesy of City of Coral Springs

Flag football is popular in the youth football program. Courtesy of City of Coral Springs

At Sherwood Forest Park the Wheel Chair Course was opened in 1986, a project of the Coral Springs Downtown Lions Club. Courtesy of City of Coral Springs

Wheelchair roadrunners compete in the ten-kilometer race. Courtesy of City of Coral Springs

Even rugby is played on occasion at Mullins Park. Courtesy of City of Coral Springs

The Honda Classic at Eagle Trace brought world-class tournament golf to Coral Springs. Courtesy of City of Coral Springs

Mayor Heafy gives the Mayor's Cup to Coral Springs High School, the winner of the annual Coral Springs-Taravella football game. Courtesy of Coral Ridge Properties

At the Honda Classic television cameras are presented with a card display creating a map of Florida. Courtesy of City of Coral Springs

Crowds follow their favorite golfers in the Honda Classic. Courtesy of City of Coral Springs

Crowd-favorite Jack Nicklaus shoots for green in 1986 Honda Classic

Eighteen thousand households are served by Cable TV of Coral Springs, a wholly owned subsidiary of Schurz Communications, Inc., of South Bend, Indiana. Cable TV first appeared in Coral Springs in the Westinghouse Electra Lab home in the early 1970s. Forty people are employed by Cable TV of Coral Springs, which has operated the service in the city since 1978. Courtesy of Cable TV of Coral Springs

Hands-across-Broward brings Coral Springs residents to the county's famed beaches. Courtesy of City of Coral Springs

The Coral Springs Police Color Guard fires a Fourth of July salute in front of the Veterans Monument. Courtesy of City of Coral Springs

Opening ceremonies signal the 1988 start of the Coral Springs girls' softball season. Courtesy of City of Coral Springs

Mai-Kai dancers make the Fourth of July an exciting holiday. Courtesy of City of Coral Springs

Coral Springs now has two synagogues for worshippers of the Jewish faith. Courtesy of City of Coral Springs

Law enforcement officer Ken Gubek and his dog, Magnum, take a break. Courtesy of City of Coral Springs

Here's looking at you, kid, Regina Levithan seems to be saying at the police department's target practice range. Courtesy of City of Coral Springs

Since 1980 the Opus Playhouse, Coral Springs' "little theater" group, has been operating out of a 230-seat playhouse on Wiles Road. The group started in 1974. Courtesy of City of Coral Springs

Chanukah, Festival of Freedom, is observed each December. Courtesy of City of Coral Springs

103

The Coral Springs Garden Club conducts a tree sale at the Coral Springs Mall. Courtesy of City of Coral Springs

Commercial development in Coral Springs shows interesting variety in its architecture. Courtesy of City of Coral Springs

New office buildings continue to rise in Coral Springs. Courtesy of City of Coral Springs

Helen Taché was the first woman elected to the Coral Springs City Commission. Courtesy of City of Coral Springs

Christian faiths are represented now in Coral Springs by fourteen churches. Courtesy of City of Coral Springs

The Sawgrass Expressway, when completed, promises improved transportation for the city of Coral Springs. Courtesy of City of Coral Springs

Coral Springs Boy Scouts observe Pioneer Days. Courtesy of City of Coral Springs

Coral Springs schools provide excellent study facilities for their students. Courtesy of City of Coral Springs

Children study in language labs in Coral Springs elementary schools. Courtesy of City of Coral Springs

Coral Springs children play at Tot Lot. Courtesy of City of Coral Springs

Graduation Day is always a major event in a city that works hard to make its schools effective. Courtesy of Coral Ridge Properties

The only planes that take off and land in Coral Springs are the model planes operated by the Condors Flying Club at Park 31 near the Sawgrass Expressway. Courtesy of City of Coral Springs

Kenny Knox glows as a victory in the 1986 Honda Classic signals an upturn in his golfing fortunes. Courtesy of City of Coral Springs

While waiting construction of a permanent Safety Town to train children, Coral Springs police devise Safety Town demonstrations of their own to teach safety. Courtesy of City of Coral Springs

The annual Easter Egg Hunt at Mullins Park is a happy event for Coral Springs children. Courtesy of City of Coral Springs

Coral Springs kids merrily look for Easter eggs at Mullins Park. Courtesy of City of Coral Springs

Kiwanis Park offers a stroll into the Florida woods via a boardwalk built by hard-working Kiwanian volunteers. Courtesy of City of Coral Springs

The Pine Ridge community has been built on land acquired in the Remsburg purchase. In the city's twenty-fifth year new homes in Coral Springs ranged from roughly $120,00 to well over a million dollars. Courtesy of Coral Ridge Properties

Bubble-blowers have their day at Mullins Park. Courtesy of City of Coral Springs

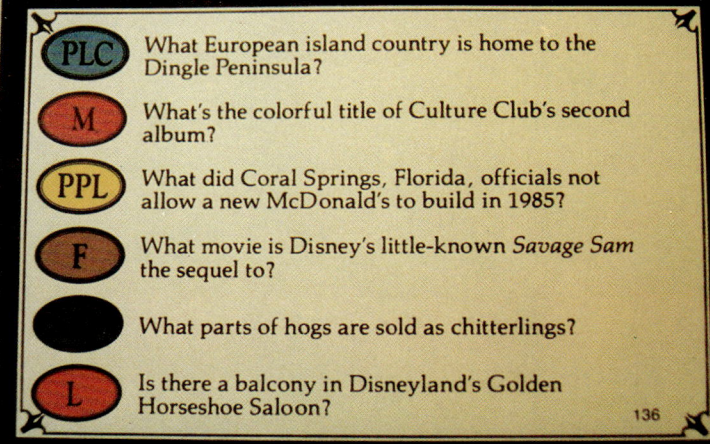

Coral Springs found its way into the Canadian version of Trivial Pursuit. "What did Coral Springs, Florida, officials not allow a new McDonald's to build in 1985?" Answer—golden arches; they ran afoul of the city strict signage code. The question, however, contains an error. McDonald's arrived in Coral Springs in 1975. Courtesy of City of Coral Springs

Flowers brighten a model row in the new Pine Ridge subdivision. Courtesy of Coral Ridge Properties

The Broken Woods golf course is now surrounded by comfortable residences. Courtesy of City of Coral Springs

Homes in Pine Ridge offer homeowners comfortable and attractive interiors. Courtesy of Coral Ridge Properties

The food tent is always a popular hangout at Our Town. Courtesy of City of Coral Springs

The Our Town festival gives families a chance to enjoy the Fun House. Courtesy of City of Coral Springs

From seventy-five feet up, the Coral Springs Fire Department demonstrates its fire-fighting prowess at Our Town. Courtesy of City of Coral Springs

Our Town, started in 1978, has become the city's major festival. *Courtesy of City of Coral Springs*

One of the features of Our Town is cheerleader competition. *Courtesy of City of Coral Springs*

At Our Town, Mayor Ben Geiger shares the spotlight with Alexandria Roumain, Miss Coral Springs of 1987. *Courtesy of City of Coral Springs*

115

Advanced powder metallurgy is used at New Industrial Techniques to fabricate parts for computers, copiers, and business machines. Here timing belt pulleys are being moved into a sintering furnace. Courtesy of New Industrial Techniques

The Taravella High School band marches in Our Town festival. Courtesy of City of Coral Springs

A Marine trumpeter blows hard at opening ceremonies at Our Town. Courtesy of City of Coral Springs

A girl stops her ears as the trumpeter plays. Courtesy of City of Coral Springs

Enjoying Our Town ceremonies are, left to right, Claire and Gordon Ickes; Jim Gordon and Don Sanders, city commissioners; Joe Titone, state representative; and Peter Weinstein, state senator. Courtesy of City of Coral Springs

Our Town draws highly competitive tug-of-war teams. Courtesy of City of Coral Springs

A happy twenty-third birthday is celebrated with the traditional cake. Left to right are Commissioners Jim Gordon and Don Sanders, Mayor Ben Geiger, Commissioner Ed Heafy, and City Manager Bill Brady. Courtesy of City of Coral Springs

The orchid holds a place of particular honor in Coral Springs. The orchid is the official city flower, the city is an orchid sanctuary, and the city has established Orchid Park. Courtesy of City of Coral Springs

The Coral Springs High School waits for the start of the Our Town parade. Courtesy of City of Coral Springs

Kids romp in plastic balls at Our Town. Courtesy of City of Coral Springs

Girl Scouts, over a thousand strong, march in Our Town parade. Courtesy of City of Coral Springs

Fans follow the play at the 1988 Honda Classic. Courtesy of City of Coral Springs

A little trouble with a sandtrap was not enough to keep Mark Calcavecchia from winning the 1987 Honda Classic at Eagle Trace. Courtesy of City of Coral Springs

In January 1988 the City of Coral Springs dedicated the new Buchanan Fire Station, named after the late Bill Buchanan, who had been an active volunteer fireman. Participating in the ribbon-cutting were Nina Buchanan, Bill's widow, and fire chief Dan Groh. Courtesy of City of Coral Springs

ELECTED AND APPOINTED OFFICIALS

MAYORS
Harry Wilson	1963-1968
Lewie Mullins	1968-1969
Robert Fuller	1969-1970
George MacGregor	1970-1972
James E. Edwards	1972-1974
O. B. "Ben" Geiger	1974-1976, 1979-1981, 1982-1990
Walter Blake	1976-1977
Ed Heafy	1977-1979, 1981-1982

VICE MAYORS
George Hammerer	1963-1965
Robert Fuller	1965
Harvey Olsen	1965-1968
Richard J. Hunt	1968-1969
Robert Fuller	1969-1970
Wilfred Neale	1970-1972
Ed Heafy	1972-1976, 1979-1980, 1982-1984, 1986-1988
Carl Zeytoonian	1976-1978
Ben Geiger	1978-1979
Helen Taché	1980-1982
Donald H. Sanders	1984-1985, 1988

CITY COMMISSIONERS
George Hammerer	1963-1965
Thomas J. Alexander	1963-1968
Harvey Olsen	1963-1965
Robert Fuller	1965, 1968-1969
Dale Hiatt	1965-1966
E. O. Knight	1965-1968
Wilfred Neale	1968-1974
Peter Giordano	1968-1970
Richard J. Hunt	1968-1972
Raymond Lopez	1969-1970
George MacGregor	1972-1974
James E. Edwards	1970-1972, 1974-1976
Ed Heafy	1970-1977, 1979-1981, 1982-1988
Walter R. Blake	1972-1976, 1977-1980
Ben Geiger	1976-1978, 1981-1982
Jack Nordlund	1974-1978
Carl Zeytoonian	1976-1984
Helen Taché	1978-1988
Donald H. Sanders	1980-1990
Timothy D. Cross	1982-1983
Jim Gordon	1983-1992
Jeanne M. Mills	1988-1990
Janet Oppenheimer	1988-1992

CITY MANAGERS
Werner Buntemeyer	1964-1974
Phillip R. Kelley	1974-1978
John A. Dow, Jr.	1978-1980
Dodd A. Southern	1980-1984
Donald Sawyer (acting city manager)	1984-1985
William B. Brady	1985-1988
Edwin A. Eddy (interim city manager)	1988

CITY CLERKS
Werner Buntemeyer	1964-1973
Jocelyn Quinn	1973
Catherine McGarity	1973-1976
Jonda K. Joseph	1976-Present

CORAL SPRINGS MILESTONES

December 14, 1961—Coral Ridge Properties buys thirty-eight hundred acres of northwest Broward County ranchland from Lena Lyons for one million dollars.

July 10, 1963—City of Coral Springs chartered by Florida Legislature.

March 21, 1965—LAND-RUSH Discount Land Sale and Barbecue held at Coral Springs.

July 9, 1965—George Knobel moves into first home sold by Coral Ridge Properties.

August 19, 1965—Harry Wilson appointed first mayor of Coral Springs by Governor Farris Bryant.

July 1, 1966—Westinghouse Electric Corporation buys Coral Ridge Properties for $36 million.

July 5, 1966—Royal Palm Boulevard dedicated to provide southern entrance into Coral Springs.

January 12, 1967—Coral Springs Chamber of Commerce organized.

January 12, 1968—Lewie Mullins becomes city's first elected mayor.

May 27, 1970—Sample Road extended to Coral Springs.

June 6, 1970—Lions Park dedicated.

October 6, 1970—Ground broken for First Presbyterian Church.

November 30, 1970—Golfers tee off in city's first PGA tournament, the Coral Springs Open.

September 12, 1972—The Bank of Coral Springs opens it doors.

January 14, 1974—Phillip R. Kelley named first fulltime city manager for Coral Springs.

February 10, 1978—City votes to buy Coral Ridge Properties Administration building for its City Hall.

March 1, 1984—Golfers tee off in first Honda Classic at Eagle Trace.

November 5, 1985—Voters approve $16 million bond program for parks, recreation, police, and fire departments and construction of community center.

February 16, 1988—City of Coral Springs completes purchase of City Hall from Coral Ridge Properties.

July 10, 1988—City of Coral Springs celebrates its twenty-fifth birthday.

INDEX

A
Aboulafia, Sol, 84
Abrams, Jennifer, 48
Abrams, Fire Chief Richard, 48
Alexander, Thomas Jarrell, 25, 121
American Snuff Company, 19
Andreotti, Eugene, 29
Atlantic Construction Company, 32
Ault, Edward, 23

B
Baker, Val, 17
Ballesteros, Seve, 56
Bank of Coral Springs, 41
Beach, Marcia, 43
Beck, Willard, 58
Beyer, Steve, 25
Blake, Mayor Walter, 40, 43, 121
Bonbrest, Bonnie, 38
Boros, Julius, 38
Brady, William N., 53, 58, 84, 85, 87, 118, 121
Brannock, Virginia, 41
Briarwood, 49, 53
Broken Woods Golf Club, 21, 23, 24, 25, 113
Broward County Archeological Society, 27, 30
Broward County Area Planning Board, 20
Broward County School Board, 34, 43
Brown, Sgt. Gary, 64
Bryant, Governor Farris, 25
Buchanan, Bill, 119
Buchanan, Nina, 119
Buntemeyer, Werner, 17, 19, 25, 34, 43, 44, 85, 121
Burns, Governor Haydon, 25
Bynum, Hal, 25

C
Cable TV of Coral Springs, 100
Cagle, Russ, 38
Calcavecchia, Mark, 55, 119
Calder, Stephen, 14
Caldwell, Jim, 47
Carson, Johnny, 22, 23
Central and Southern Florida Flood Control District, 17, 38
Chadwick, David, 78
Challenger Time Capsule, 66
Collier, George, 19
Connor, Chuck, 47
Connors, Dorothy, 25
Coral Ridge Properties, 14, 15, 17, 19, 20, 22, 25, 27, 30, 38, 41, 44, 47, 53, 54, 55, 58, 79, 85
Coral Ridge Properties Administration Building/Coral Springs City Hall, 25-27, 44, 49, 58, 79, 81, 90
Coral Savings and Loan Association, 58
Coral Savings Centre, 58, 81
Coral Springs Chamber of Commerce, 21, 25, 34, 37
Coral Springs Chronicle, 40
Coral Springs Country Club, 23, 33, 38, 81, 96
Coral Springs Elementary School, 38
Coral Springs Financial Plaza, 51, 63
Coral Springs Fire Department, 36, 41, 44, 48, 59, 63, 70, 78, 114
Coral Springs Forum, 40
Coral Springs Garden Club, 104
Coral Springs Hebrew Congregation, 41
Coral Springs High School, 44, 46, 47, 83, 98, 118
Coral Springs Historical Society, 41
Coral Springs Library, 41, 53, 54
Coral Springs Mall, 44, 50, 51, 81, 104
Coral Springs Medical Center, 56, 68, 71
Coral Springs Monthly, 40
Coral Springs News, 40
Coral Springs Open, 38, 51
Coral Springs Parent-Teacher Organization, 38, 40
Coral Springs Police Department, 24, 25, 29, 40, 41, 60, 64, 82, 101, 110
Coral Springs, population, 23, 34, 56, 81

Coral Springs Post Office, 25, 41
Coral Springs Sunrise Towers, 56, 57
Coral Springs Teen Association, 40
Coral Square Mall, 54, 57
Country Club Tower, 44, 81
Covered Bridge, 18, 19, 20, 80
Cross, Timothy, 121
Cubillas, Teofilo, 78
Cummings, Jan, 43
Curran, William, 17

D
Dogs, 41, 76, 102
Dorsey, George, 34
Dow, John A., Jr., 53, 121
Ducharme, King, 38

E
Eagle Trace, 20, 47, 55, 56, 67
Eddy, Edwin A., 121
Edwards, James, 34, 40, 121
Edward J. DeBartolo Company, 54, 57
Eveker, Don, 44, 70
Ezratti, Itchko, 57

F
Facterman, Linda, 77
Faldo, Nick, 56
First Presbyterian Church, 38
Fisher, Louis, 14
Floyd, Raymond, 56
Florida Parent Magazine, 58
Foltz, Dennis, 81
Ford, President Gerald, 47, 56
Fort Lauderdale Strikers, 48
Fowles, Colin, 78
Frazier, H.J., 54, 55
Freerks, Mark, 34, 35
Fuller, Robert, J., 19, 25, 38, 121

G
Galt, Arthur, 14
Galt Ocean Mile Hotel, 18, 22
Gardner, Jack, 11
Gardner, Sandi, 64
Garrett, Bill, 38, 55
Geiger, Mayor O. B. "Ben", 43, 44, 48, 49, 56, 62, 87, 118, 121
Gilbert, Chief Warren, 61, 69, 81, 86
Giordano, Peter, 25, 121
Gleason, Jackie, 55
Gordon, Diane, 41
Gordon, James, 53, 79, 117, 118, 121
Gosselin, Raul, 38
Graham, Reverend Billy, 58
Gray, Col. Ralph, 36
Groh, Chief Dan, 79, 119
Grossjung, Thomas L., 56
Gubek, Ken, 102

H
Hammerer, George W., 25, 121
Hanrahan, Sgt. Jim, 60, 64
Hardiman, Peter, 58
Hartford, Bob, 21
Heafy, Ed, 34, 38, 40, 43, 44, 48, 49, 58, 64, 79, 98, 118, 121
Heafy, Jennifer, 70
Henderson, Randy, 64
Hills, Art, 55
Hodapp, George, 17, 18, 20, 43, 55, 79
Hodges, Draper H., 41
Hofmann, Robert, 14, 38, 41, 48, 49, 57
Holiday Inn, 44, 51, 81, 86
Holtsclaw, Bob, 67
Honda Classic, 55, 56, 98, 99, 118
Hugins, Al, 47
Hunt, James S., 13, 14, 15, 17, 18, 19, 23, 27, 41, 47, 55, 56, 58, 81
Hunt, Richard J., 25, 34, 121
Hunt Elementary School, 41

I
Ickes, Claire, 117
Ickes, Gordon, 16, 17, 18, 27, 85, 87, 117
Ingold, Carol, 74
Irwin, Hale, 56

J
Jacobsen, Peter, 55, 59

K
Kelley, Phillip R., 44, 48, 49, 53, 121
Kite, Tom, 56
Kiwanis Park, 112
Knight, E. O. (Chubby), 22, 121
Knobel, George, 23
Knox, Kenny, 111

L
Land sales, 18, 19, 21, 22, 23
Langer, Bernhard, 56
Larsen, Betty, 37
Lauderdale, Countess of (see Gwendolyn Maitland)
Levithan, Regina, 102
Lietzke, Bruce, 55
Lions Park, 36, 37
Little League Baseball, 46, 77
Lombardo, Guy, 22
Lopez, Raymond, 29, 121
Lyle, Sandy, 56
Lyons, Church, 15
Lyons, Henry L. "Bud," 13, 14
Lyons, Lena, 14, 15, 18, 19, 56

M
McCormick, Bernard, 58
McDonald's, 56
McDonough, Paul, 43, 44, 49
MacGregor, George, 34, 38, 43, 121
MacGregor, Janet, 43
McElderry, Suzanne, 40
McRoberts, Flynn, 85
Maitland, Gwendolyn, 14
Maplewood Elementary School, 84
Marketeer, 37, 38
Miami Herald, 85, 87
Mills, Jeanne, 58, 79, 84, 87, 121
Mini Museum, 41
Mitchell, Astronaut Gordon, 43
Montayne, Carlton (Monty), 21, 25
Morgen, Ralph, 41
Mucci, Jerry, 44
Mullins, Caroline, 25
Mullins, Lewie, 19, 20, 25, 29, 121
Mullins Park, 27, 29, 40, 42, 44, 58, 66, 67, 71, 73, 76, 91, 92, 93, 97, 112
Murch, Phil, 83
Murphy, Bob, 38

N
National City Bank, 57
National Maritime Union, 17
Neale, Wilfred, 25, 29, 34, 43, 121
Nekich, John, 36
New Industrial Techniques, 29, 116
Newman, Ron, 48
Nicholson, Pat, 43
Nicklaus, Jack, 99
Nolan, Mrs. Douglas, 34, 37
Nordlund, Jack, 46, 48, 121
Norman, Greg, 62
Nova University, 44
Novotny, James, 17, 18, 20
Novotny, David, 17

O
Olsen, Harvey, Jr., 25, 28, 121
Oppenheimer, Janet, 58, 79, 121
Opus Playhouse, 103
Orchid Park, 115
Our Town, 50, 75, 77, 88, 114, 115, 116, 117, 118

P
Palmer, Arnold, 38, 39, 51
Park of Industry, 25, 27, 30, 44, 81
Pezoldt, Kenneth W., 25
Pine Ridge, 112, 113
Platt, George, 43
Porter, George, 17, 19, 20
Powell, Carol, 41
Proffitt, Paul, 47
Publix Supermarket, 33

Q
Quad City News, 41

R
Ramblewood Middle School, 82
Ray, Berry, 38
Reagan, President Ronald, 48

Red Fox Inn, 28
Reiss, Dorothy, 41
Remsburg, Luther, 38
Reynolds, Bert, 55
Reynolds, Debbie, 42
Robbie, Elizabeth, 48
Rogers, Mary, 83
Rogers, Congressman Paul, 34, 37, 44, 48
Roumain, Alexandria, 118
Rowe, Russell, 38, 40
Ruffalo, Mario, 94-95
Russell, George, 25
Russian Home, 32

S
Saddle Club, 36
Safety Town, 110
Salzer, E. A., 57
Sample Road, 27, 38, 52
Sanders, Donald, 53, 56, 62, 64, 79, 117, 118, 121
Sanders, Yvette, 62
Sartory, Virginia, 43
Sawgrass Expressway, 56, 81, 106
Sawyer, Donald, 53, 121
Schechter, Stuart, 57
Schwabe, Chuck, 11
Sherwood Forest, 96
Shirnpf, Fred, 19
Siano, Lou, 67
Sindelar, Joey, 55
Singer, Jan, 37
Singer, Paul, 38
Smith, Jeannie, 38
Smokey and the Bandit, Part 3, 34, 35
Soccer, 48, 78, 72
Sosnowsky, Carl, 61
Southern Regional Baseball Tournament, 64, 91
Southern, Dodd A., 53, 121
Sproule, William, 57
Stadler, Craig, 56
Stafford, Nancy, 49
Stanley, Byron, 64
Strange, Curtis, 55, 59
Sullivan, Helene, 37
Sunshine Drainage District, 17, 19

T
Taché, Helen, 47, 48, 58, 79, 121
Taravella, Joseph, 14, 27, 34, 36, 38, 44, 46, 47, 82, 105
Taravella High School, 82, 98, 116
Taylor, Marina, 41
Tequesta Indians, 27
Tisdale, Mrs. Charles, 34
Titone, Joe, 43, 117
Tournament Players Club, 55
Trevino, Lee, 38
Trivial Pursuit, 118
Trout, John, 57
Twaddell, Kenneth, 48

U
University Drive, 18

V
Varvoutis, Alice, 34
Vedilago, Richard, 24, 25, 29
Village Green Shopping Center, 27, 35, 54
Village Square Shopping Center, 41, 44, 54

W
Weber, Carol, 87
Weiskopf, Tom, 56
Weinstein, Sen. Peter, 43, 117
Welborn, Max, 19
Welcome Wagon Club, 40, 41, 53
Westinghouse Electric Corp., 25, 27, 30, 32, 36, 39, 41, 42, 43, 54
Westinghouse Relay Telecommunications Division, 44, 50, 75
Wiles Road, 15, 19, 36, 56
Williams, Paul, 55
Williams, Wilma, 27
Wilson, Mayor Harry, 22, 25, 121

Z
Zeytoonian, Carl, 48, 121

123

ABOUT THE AUTHOR

Photo by Peter Colelli

Stuart McIver, author, editor, and screenwriter, has written four books and more than two hundred articles on Florida history. His honors include the Florida Historical Confederation's first annual Award of Merit for historical writing; in addition he has written scripts for documentary films which have won two CINE Golden Eagles and one Silver Medal at the Venice Film Festival. He serves as co-editor of *Update*, the quarterly publication of the Historical Association of Southern Florida and the Caribbean; as president of the Book Group of South Florida, an organization of Florida authors and publishers; and is a director of the Florida Historical Society.